Your Towns and Cities in the Great War

Wellington

in the Great War

Your Towns and Cities in the Great War

Wellington

in the Great War

by Christopher W. A. Owen

Pen & Sword
MILITARY

First published in Great Britain in 2016 by
PEN & SWORD MILITARY
an imprint of
Pen and Sword Books Ltd
47 Church Street
Barnsley
South Yorkshire S70 2AS

ISBN 978 1 78346 3 541

A CIP record for this book is available from the British Library

Printed and bound in England
by CPI Group (UK) Ltd, Croydon, CR0 4YY

Pen & Sword Books Ltd incorporates the imprints of
Pen & Sword Archaeology, Atlas, Aviation, Battleground, Discovery,
Family History, History, Maritime, Military, Naval, Politics, Railways,
Select, Social History, Transport, True Crime, and Claymore Press,
Frontline Books, Leo Cooper, Praetorian Press, Remember When,
Seaforth Publishing and Wharncliffe.

For a complete list of Pen and Sword titles please contact
Pen and Sword Books Limited
47 Church Street, Barnsley, South Yorkshire, S70 2AS, England
E-mail: enquiries@pen-and-sword.co.uk
Website: www.pen-and-sword.co.uk

Contents

Dedication

This book is dedicated to the 182 battle fatalities suffered by Wellington in the Great War and also the long-term casualties who fought on behalf of the town and the surrounding area. These were the brave men and women who survived the carnage only to endure permanently disabling physical and mental injuries.

Regrettably none of the survivors, with some rare exceptions, appear on any official war memorials, local or national. The ultimate sacrifice was made by the young people of Wellington who thought they were fighting a necessary and just 'war to end all wars'. Their testaments indicate that, in their hearts, each one genuinely believed that by their diligent service to the nation, future kith and kin would never have to face such a catastrophe ever again. They gave their lives willingly to the cause - not just for King and country but in the name of freedom from tyranny.

For that reason, if no other, we should remember them forever.

Chris Owen
July 2016

Foreword

By Councillor Karen Tomlinson Mayor of Wellington – September 2014:

'I invite you to take this book and immerse yourself in it. As you read, think about the local men and women whose lives have been touched by this terrible war. Think about the consequences they suffered. Then ask yourself the ultimate questions.'

Acknowledgements

To those parties and organisations listed below without whose help and support this book would not have been possible:-

- Allan Frost, local historian and author, for use of period photos and inclusion of factual material from his book *The Great War in Wellington*.

- George Evans, local author and peace gardener, for personal contributions.

- Shropshire Archives for access to newspaper articles and local maps.

- Toby Neal, journalist, *Shropshire Star*, local historian and author, for use of period photos, archive material and leads to personal stories.

- Shropshire Regimental Museum, Shrewsbury, for information about the KSLI.

- Martin Scholes, journalist, *Wrekin News* for cover photo and other materials.

- Wellington Library for access to archives facilities such as *The Wellington Journal*.

- Arleston Memories Group, especially Councillor Angela McClements and David Barnett.

- Mervyn Joyner, Chief Archivist Wrekin College for pertinent materials.

- Howard Perkins, Wellington Town Clerk for help and civic materials including kind permission to reproduce the town crest.

- Councillor Karen Tomlinson, Mayor of Wellington, for co-operation and material contributions.

- Royal Befordshire Regiment for online war diary extracts.

- Mr. Martin M. Stott, Headmaster, The Old Hall School for material contributions and access to memorial plaques, reproduced by kind permission.

- Wellington History Group for help and honorary membership enabling me to access Shropshire archives.

- All the relatives of Wellington's First World War service personnel who gave permission to include their stories and to reproduce personal letters and relevant documentation.

A Brief Introduction to the Great War (1914 - 1918)

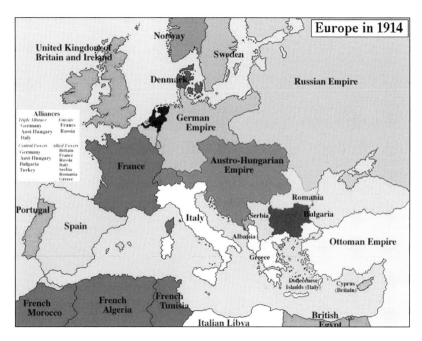

Diagrammatic map of Europe in 1914 showing military alliances

It is now more than a century since the outbreak of 'The Great War' as it was dubbed by those who fought in it and those who died in it. None of them could have known, or even suspected, that it was to become a world-changing cataclysmic event with repercussions affecting, not just the combatant nations throughout the war and in its aftermath, but most facets of society – even up to present day.

Europe at the time was a melting pot of intrigue and empire building where the great nations were far too busy bickering amongst themselves to realize the magnitude of the tragedy they were to unleash. The political cauldron was coming to the boiling point with only one single spark required to light the blue touchpaper of war. The various treaties and alliances helped factionalize opposition in a Europe where, for example, France formalised relations with Britain via the *Entente Cordiale* signed in 1904. This was a formal agreement to protect one another's territorial interests if threatened. In 1907 Russia, fearing German expansion – particularly in the eastern states and the Balkans – joined them to form the Grand or Triple Alliance. Meanwhile Germany, acting in self-defence, formed the central powers alliance with Austro-Hungary, Italy, Bulgaria and later, Turkey. The spark needed to ignite the Great War came in the form of a brutal assassination born out of a pre-existing conflict a thousand miles away from British shores, inside the Balkans.

This was a politically unstable region that had suffered several small, localised wars for three years leading up to the First World War in order to free itself from the yoke of the Austro-Hungarian Empire. Kaiser Wilhelm II of Germany used this single incident as a convenient ruse to trigger a considerably greater conflict.

When hostilities broke out, the warring nations, including Britain, very quickly found themselves presiding over an expensive and protracted disaster. The war began in the latter half of 1914 and was contested for over four long and bloody years up to the final quarter of 1918. Most nations had anticipated that it would be over and done within a much shorter time frame, as both sides believed the loser would sue for peace very quickly (in months, not years) rather than face the consequences of humiliating defeat.

Kaiser Wilhelm II -
Germany's leader and ruler

The Great War was expensive for the UK in terms of the loss of life, both civilian and military, which comprised largely the youthful flower of a generation and affected one in eight families across the nation. It was protracted because the result of similarly matched opposing forces was inevitable stalemate. This position was further aggravated by a stubborn reluctance on both sides to negotiate a peaceful settlement, even after the pitched land battles began to take a terrible toll on their respective armies for very small territorial gains. Each and every nation was driven by the foolhardy conviction that it was pursuing a just and righteous cause by fighting 'a war to end all wars'.

Even the Germans believed passionately that they would prevail in their support of the Kaiser's mad military quest for territorial gains because plainly God was on their side.

As the casualties mounted on both sides, Britain and her Allies were also convinced of divine support. Their fight became a crusade to rid the world of German oppression.

Wellington's casualties alone are put at 182 out of a national death toll of 1.3 million servicemen and women (including Commonwealth forces) with thousands more missing in action or with no known grave.

The war was expensive for the UK in money terms, resulting in a post-war national debt exceeding an economy-busting 13 billion pounds. Whilst some nations, such as the USA, emerged stronger politically and economically in the aftermath, the Great War was to leave Great Britain, a once powerful industrial and colonial nation, bankrupt, financially and emotionally.

Given the scale of the tragedy and its consequences, the First World War could arguably be termed the single most defining moment in the political and social roadmap of the twentieth century. Never before had our world witnessed such a comprehensive and universal catastrophe. Once-great European dynasties, which had ruled for hundreds of years, were toppled during the war's course changing forever the social, economical and political destiny of several countries, including Germany. In consequence, this pivotal event in the closing century of the second millennium, spawned an even more devastating war in its wake.

Other resultant political, territorial and social repercussions of the Great War still affect our world today. Particularly relevant is the upsurge of Middle Eastern terrorism born largely out of inequitable territorial designations enshrined in the Versailles peace treaty provisions of 1919. These damaging mandatory terms were arbitrarily imposed by the victors upon the losers (Germany and her allies) without consensual agreement. In most cases it rewrote the map of Europe and perhaps more crucially the Middle East.

The Great War was also a seminal conflict unique in its devolved historical and political circumstances, its mass implementation of technological innovation and the scale of its global prosecution across land, sea and latterly the air. However, it is now remembered mostly for its appalling casualty statistics.

In this book we will attempt to tell the story of the little market town of Wellington and its inhabitants whose extraordinary sacrifice for this conflict is all the the more remarkable given its replication in similar towns and communities across the length and breadth of Britain. This was mainly due to the outpouring of mass patriotism born out of a sense of national pride. It was exploited further by a spectacular and uniquely British newspaper and poster advertising campaign that captured the nation's hearts and minds.

Utilising a now famous depiction of the national war hero, Lord Horatio Herbert Kitchener, coupled with bold jingoistic sentiments to motivate the eligible populace to enlist in the service of King and country, it was to yield rapid and vast numerical results.

During the early part of the twentieth century leading up to the Great War, the UK was admired and envied, particularly by Germany, for being a powerful industrial and colonial empire.

Lord Horatio Herbert Kitchener, Secretary of State for War and Chief of the Army 1914

Archduke Franz Ferdinand, circa 1914

Wellington's townsfolk responded dutifully when their young men (and latterly women) were called for war service to defend the realm from foreign aggressors. Germany, under its Kaiser, was to be vilified as the chief instigator of the war, yet never sought to involve other countries such as Britain. It believed the UK would view any conflict in Europe as a petty squabble and keep out of it. It also believed the UK and her Allies would never honour treaty obligations in Europe (which in the case of Belgium had stood since 1839) to the point of actually declaring war. After all Kaiser Wilhelm II was family; a grandson of the late Queen Victoria who was in turn grandmother to the reigning British monarch, Wilhelm's cousin, King George V. The distant rumblings of war were brought sharply into focus by the events of 28 June 1914 when the heir to the Austro-Hungarian empire Archduke Franz Ferdinand, was assassinated along with his wife whilst on a state visit to Sarajevo, the capital of Bosnia and Herzegovina.

Germany's Kaiser Wilhelm II capitalised on this and it became the spark that lit the touchpaper that started the war. The terrorist actions of the Bosnian Serb assassin Gavrilo Princip provided the Kaiser with the perfect excuse to persuade Austro-Hungary to declare war on Serbia.

She in turn influenced Bosnia and all the Serb nations in the Balkans, who sought freedom from the long, oppressive reign of the Austro-Hungarian empire, to fight.

The declaration of war drew Russia directly into the conflict to defend the interests of a fellow Slavic nation, as it was obliged by treaty to do so.

Germany had already started implementing its master war plan, devised by its Chief of Staff Count Alfred von Schlieffen, who did not live to see it come to fruition.

This pre-war strategy of 1907 was designed to subjugate France within six weeks by invading via neutral Belgium in order to sweep round from the western outskirts of Paris to surround its army centred on Verdun, located on its north-eastern border with Germany.

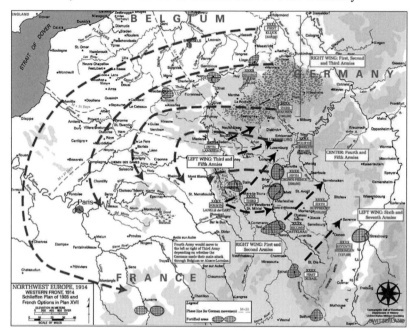

Diagrammatic map of the Von Schlieffen Plan

Although now forced to fight the war on two fronts, Germany was confident of success. It was able to act boldly in the belief that Britain would not honour its 1839 treaty with Belgium, to protect both its neutrality and defend its sovereignty if invaded.

Coupled with some weak leadership from the Belgian monarch King Albert and a miniscule army of 40,000 regulars, Belgium suffered fighting from day one to the very last on its own soil and was rendered powerless to fend off this invasion. Being an autocratic ruler, a position he enforced ruthlessly, Kaiser Wilhelm's appointment of key ministers and senior army officers was based mainly on intuition, favouritism and bullying tactics. His idiosyncratically flawed approach to managing fundamental strategic planning, subverted by some rogue generals, would ultimately lose Germany the war.

We will also contrast the Home Front with the war effort and show how the spirit of the Wellington townspeople was influenced by shameless national propaganda, largely espoused by Herbert Asquith, who as Foreign Secretary prior to the war, stated: 'Germany covets our naval and colonial world status and if they declare war on us we will give them a bloody nose and send them packing within the first six months.'

Herbert Asquith - circa 1914

This flawed jingoistic advice motivated over 1.4 million young men nationwide, including those from Wellington, to enlist as Lord Kitchener's volunteers, within the first eighteen months of the outbreak.

Many were formed into 'Pals' battalions' comprising groups of friends or workmates who enlisted together for the very big and very short adventure.They were assured by the Army, the government and the press that it would all be over in six months because Germany was ill-equipped and no match for the might of the British forces. Indeed they were considered invincible having not lost any foreign or European wars for over a century. However the Great War turned into a prolonged disaster, devastating whole communities such as Wellington's in the process. The sudden influx of enlistees swelled the number of the British Army from 247,000 regulars plus 213,000 reservists at the outbreak in 1914, to over two million men by 1915. This meant the infantry now largely comprised volunteer citizen soldiery lacking fieldcraft skills and battleground experience. Inevitably this exposed them as raw, inexperienced recruits who were perilously ill-equipped to cope with unrelenting warfare on such a vast scale. This was a fate shared by their commanding officers who failed to cope with the logistics of handling an astronomical amount of men in the field. Disastrous infantry losses meant numbers were so depleted by the end of 1915 that compulsory conscription was introduced in March 1916. It was surprising that Britain reacted so poorly to the impending threat of war in Europe.

Given the explosive pressure-cooker mix that plagued politics immediately prior to the outbreak and despite all the treaty agreements protecting them, not one European country, including Britain, had implemented or even discussed any contingency plans.

This would have ensured the co-ordination of their respective forces on a prolonged and sustainable basis long before they were welded together to form what was to be called the Allies. This was a loose term for a military confederation comprising all the nations fighting Germany for the duration. Even Germany's allies' were much more organized and of greater strength than Britain's. The lax peacetime policies of government and blatant overconfidence in her naval strength had resulted in a depletion of land forces before the outbreak of the First World War. By comparison, France, Britain's closest ally, had 800,000 trained regulars and Russia boasted over a million men in uniform. Germany had almost 500,000 experienced and well-equipped regular soldiers in its Imperial Army termed *Kaiserheer* and thousands of trained reservists to call on in time of war, as national service was extended up to the age of 45.

On the British Home Front draconian wartime legislation was introduced quickly, designed to control every aspect of people's lives in the name of national security.

The Defence of the Realm Act 1914 (DORA) was to destroy numerous small businesses nationally and, as the local paper, the *Wellington Journal and Shrewsbury News* reported, several of those similar businesses were based in the town itself. The government's sweeping powers not only drastically affected how trade was conducted but also the source of its lifeblood: horses and the manpower to work them were both now requisitioned for King and country. The resultant manpower shortages led to the establishment of an entirely new working class.

Previously in the UK, women fulfilled the traditional roles of homemakers, stay-at-home mothers and wives to male workers who now turned into soldiers in uniform for the duration of the war. The great Liberal Party politician of the day, David Lloyd George, almost single-handedly galvanised businessmen and fought off trade union opposition to employ women in vast numbers in various trades – particularly engineering. This was the linchpin of his campaign to urge Britain to fight a 'total war' against Germany in order to ensure victory. As working women's income increased they were able to put more meat and fresh food on the table thus allowing diets to improve. This allowed poorer people access to various foodstuffs previously denied to them.

Women were paid more for industrial work than they were for shop work or domestic service and were instrumental in transforming UK industrial capacity and output, in particular the supply of battlefront munitions. Wellington and the surrounding areas of Lilleshall, Priorslee, Hadley and nearby Coalbrookdale in Ironbridge, were to play their part in this new development.

We will discover the great compassion shown by Wellington people who sheltered Belgian war refugees at a time of national crisis. Britain could have become insular in its outlook to foreigners given the nature and structure of its society. Its myriad prejudices concerning class and ethnicity were deeply rooted at the time. Nevertheless this heartfelt gesture from the British as well as the French nations was appreciated deeply and it is remembered by the Belgian people to this day. Unfortunately as the war dragged on, the extent of the reprisals following German naval bombardments of North East coastal towns as well as successive air raids carried out by Zeppelin airships and latterly Gotha heavy bombers, resulted in the eruption of mindless violence in the UK. This was meted out to anyone of German nationality or descent regardless of whether they had resided in the UK for years before the war was even conceived, let alone commenced.

We will record the deprivation caused by the loss of manpower and animal resources to the Wellington community aggravated by mysterious pseudo-military tribunals brought in to enforce the heinous conscription laws. These laws were introduced in panicked reaction to the falling infantry numbers caused by appalling slaughter in that theatre of war called the Western Front. This was attributed largely to an inflexible military strategy amounting to incompetence on the part of the commanding generals. The waste of infantry soldiers on the battlefields of Flanders came to typify the carnage involved thus coining the expression: 'lions led by donkeys'.

The early battles resulted in stalemate by the end of 1914 producing

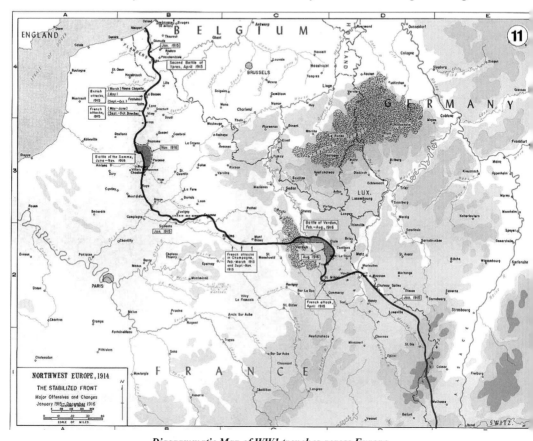

Diagrammatic Map of WW1 trenches across Europe

a static war fought along a line of trenches extending 600km from the Belgian coast across Northern France to the Swiss border.

Trench warfare was not a new tactic and set the war back several hundred years to a time when siege mentality prevailed. It was a simple way of securing a lengthy frontline that could be lightly manned. Trenches were constructed in a Greek key, or zig-zag, pattern interspersed with blockhouses every few hundred yards for use as company command posts, barracks or machine gun posts.

This meant that any enemy breakthrough could be dealt with

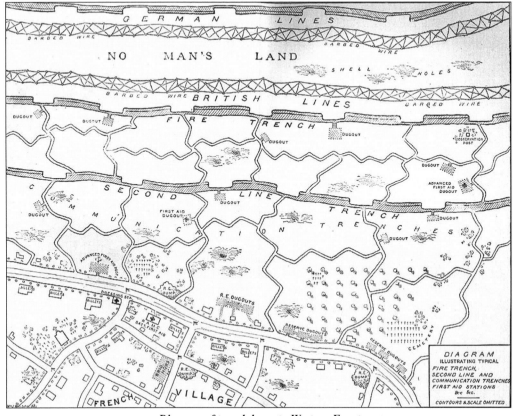

Diagram of trench layout - Western Front

sectionally and artillery blasts were confined to smaller areas causing minimal damage.

Frontline trench duty was usually limited to seven days after which time troops were withdrawn to a rest area behind the line where they could shower, launder uniforms and generally refresh themselves. They were then stood down for a month or six weeks before being rotated back to the front. Plenty of time for an infantryman to acclimatize himself for warfare.

The Germans later developed the second line network of trenches that made their defences much more unassailable thereby prolonging hostilities further.

As the war that was promised to last only six months dragged on, the stream of eager volunteers dried up. Even the patriotic young men of Wellington realized that what they were being asked to join was no short adventure with some pals followed by a big boozy reunion back home.

It was turning into a long and bloody fight in which they were more than likely to lose their lives or even worse – suffer permanent disability. For when these men returned home critically injured with no structured aftercare or antibiotics to ward off secondary infections they frequently succumbed to their wounds. Worse awaited those who survived the war physically intact. Some combat veterans suffered variations of what we would now call battle fatigue or post traumatic stress disorder (PTSD). Although recognised by First World War clinicians who termed it 'shell shock', most sufferers were ridiculed openly as cowards and malingerers, effectively shamed if they were afflicted by the condition. Some men even returned to the trenches to resume fighting duties despite being severely disabled and at risk to others and to themselves, particularly when handling weapons. Medical staff were pressured into declaring these men fit for duty even though they knew their true state of health. Consequently men who served rarely discussed their experiences of war with family or friends and simply rebuilt their lives as best they could to try and help them forget the horrors they witnessed.

We will also cover the relevant story of the rise and fall of the King's Shropshire Light Infantry (KSLI), a famous regiment founded in Shropshire, which held recruiting sway in Wellington and the West Midlands during the Great War. Although administered from its Shrewsbury headquarters it absorbed elements of the proud Shropshire Yeomanry with which it merged reluctantly during the war.

We will detail the concept of Britain's unique 'Home Front', which created a citizens' army in Wellington called the Volunteer Civilian Corps (a forerunner to the Home Guard in the Second World War) and also turned a nationally respected youth group into a force of local spies.

We will also recount the convalescence of Wellington's war wounded and the enormous outpouring of philanthropy that resulted in the founding of local hospital accommodation. This was equipped to ensure they had the best care available, long before the institution of the welfare state. The overwhelming number of casualties swamped the UK's main hospitals and so suitable buildings were requisitioned by the War Office. These were largely adapted premises such as public access buildings and cottage hospitals and were staffed mostly by volunteer nurses. In the main these were termed convalescent hospitals as it was deemed necessary to turn casualties around as quickly as possible and get them back to the front as fighting units, sometimes regardless of the severity of their wounds. The average stay varied from seven days to three weeks, with return to duty seen as the priority. Kindly and compassionate treatment was all very well but serving the national interest came first.

We will also look at how Wellington commemorated its dead in the aftermath and also the terrible legacy of the war, which afflicted the whole of British society beyond the Second World War, even to the present day. Wellington was no different from other towns as it would pay a price for contributing its best blood to fight for King and country in the Great War.

Yet all of this lay ahead as Wellingtonians basked in the lengthy bank holiday summer sunshine of 1914, blissfully unaware of their fate.

Distant Rumblings of Great Events

'The great clock chimed and we all felt the hammer of doom ringing in our ears' (Prime Minister David Lloyd George on the countdown to the war's declaration marked by Big Ben at 11.00 pm GMT on Tuesday, 4 August 1914, midnight in Berlin)

A Brief Description of Wellington Town and its History

Street view of Wellington

Wellington town crest

The town of Wellington in Shropshire (population 25,000 and rising) is located at the Western terminus of the M54 motorway (which in turn branches off the M6 motorway northbound) twelve miles north west of Wolverhampton.

Shropshire is mostly a vast farming county bordering mid Wales and the town lies at the southerly edge of its great plain, adjoining a famous landmark called the Wrekin Hill, which nestles alongside its sibling mount The Ercall. The larger sibling is namechecked in the famous saying: 'all around the Wrekin', which means someone who is prevaricating or failing to explain something clearly and succinctly.

The town's name is said to derive from the Anglo Saxon 'Weola', the name of a local Saxon settler who established his farmstead somewhere near the centre, possibly at the Church Green, on which stands All Saints Church, home to the Lych Gate Memorial.

A church has stood in Wellington, at or near this spot, for over 1,000 years and one of the associated clergy is mentioned in the Domesday Book.

Wellington All Saints Church

Wellington has been a chartered market town since AD 1244, having been granted to the local lord, Giles of Erdington, by the royal decree of King Henry III, also known as Henry of Winchester (1207 - 1272 AD).

In March, the town marks Charter Day, which was when the royal charter was delivered by a messenger on horseback. In keeping with tradition, a ceremonial jury convenes in Market Square to appoint the town crier, ale taster and market clerk for the year ahead.

In 1642 as civil war raged across England it was said King Charles stayed overnight near the town while on his way from Newport to Shrewsbury to rally support and confer honours for cash to raise an army to fight Cromwell's parliamentarian forces.

Whilst here he made his famous Wellington Declaration promising to protect the laws of England, the Protestant religion and the freedom of Parliament.

Wellington Market was built around 1680 and existed as an open-sided hall containing stalls that were demolished in 1805. After that it was held twice weekly on Church Green with open stalls that lined Church Street. The structure we still see in Market Street today was erected and opened in 1864.

Wellington Market main entrance today

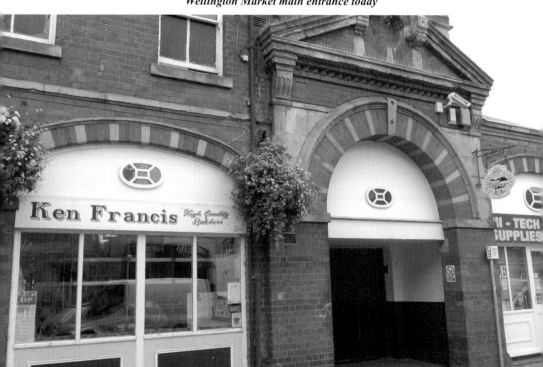

Hesba Stretton

It could be said that Wellington had a checkered history economically and politically speaking. Up to the twentieth century it was a bustling, prosperous and vibrant independent community served by a mainline railway station, which opened in 1848.

This innovative form of transport was the key to diversifying and expanding trade and helped local businesses develop rapidly.

The railway transported agricultural goods and livestock to larger markets in the Midlands and in doing so local companies grew. These included S. Corbett & Son, ironmongers and agricultural engineers who manufactured tools, hoes, seed drills and ploughs. Barber & Son (now an estate agents) established circa 1850 were livestock traders who ran the twice weekly livestock market off Bridge Road (now a supermarket site) adjoining the old stockyards alongside the rail link that serviced large cities such as Birmingham via Wolverhampton.

Tourism also began to flourish in Wellington as it was seen as an ideal place to stop off and visit landmarks such as the Wrekin, before the great trek westwards to historic destinations such as Shrewsbury and beyond to the Welsh coastal resort of Aberystwyth.

It can also lay claim to be the birthplace of numerous nineteenth century luminaries such as the Victorian novelist Hesba Stretton (1832–1911), as well as physician, botanist and herbalist Doctor William Withering, who was born in Wellington in 1741 and was a member of the famous Lunar Society. His pioneering work helped in the

William Withering

Poet Philip Larkin

discovery of the drug digitalis as an aid in the treatment of some heart conditions.

Latterly in the twentieth century, Wellington was the workplace of the poet Philip Larkin who was employed as the town's head librarian from 1943 to 1945. Of his stay, he said: 'that it was spent endlessly dishing out trashy novels to morons.'

Wellington has enjoyed its own administrative autonomy for generations having its own civic structure comprising an elected mayor and town council, which it retains to this day.

However Wellington is now a town in the unitary authority of Telford and Wrekin, in the ceremonial county of Shropshire and it forms part of the new town of Telford.

In this respect it shares the same fate as other world-famous local towns and villages, notably Ironbridge – birthplace of the modern iron and steel industry – and Coalport whose ceramics company (part of the Wedgwood group) was the originator of fine bone china. Both towns are situated a short distance away alongside the river Severn, a mighty artery of commerce for hundreds of years.

Even up to the outbreak of the Great War, Wellington enjoyed diverse economic prosperity. Based mainly around agriculture, the economy thrived on farm machinery supply and the trading of livestock at a bustling weekly market selling farming implements as well as horses, which were the main beasts of burden and provided the motive-power for all the agricultural machinery prior to the war. The town had an independent weekly newspaper called *The Wellington Journal* (latterly merged with the *Shrewsbury News*), which published every Saturday and had offices based in Church Street.

During that long hot summer of 1914 Wellington busied itself with its usual preoccupations, continuing to work, study and play as it had done for generations. Indeed the day before war was announced on 4 August and even up to the declaration on that sunny Tuesday, Britain enjoyed an extended bank holiday instigated by the government to avoid a run on the banks. Thankful and blissfully unaware of any political machinations, Wellingtonians had enjoyed a gymnastics display given by the King's Shropshire Light Infantry (KSLI) and held in the grounds of Wellington College (renamed Wrekin College in 1921).

We cannot help but speculate how many of these young gymnasts survived the imminent and bloody conflict that was about to engulf them.

Wellington's inhabitants gave no particular thought to the monumental events unfolding across the English Channel in Europe and around the globe.

Events that were to overwhelm Wellington families and leave their indelible mark on this little Shropshire community dubbed 'Wrekin Town' – forever.

KSLI gymnastics display, 3 August 1914

How News of the Outbreak of War Reached Wellington

News of the war's declaration was read to the gathered public from an upper window of the Wrekin Hotel in Market Square on Saturday, 8 August 1914.

All news was broadcast via national and local newspapers and in Wellington's case through the pages of *The Journal*'s Saturday edition published that same day. It was four days after the declaration of war made by the British Government under Herbert Asquith's premiership. Amazingly it didn't make page one as it would today but only merited a page six position, which is where all war news could be found for a good period of time. It demonstrates what little importance these events held for the average person in the heady, early days of the war, even up until the horrors of the Somme.

Wellington Market Square, circa 1914 – Courtesy of **The Journal**

A Local Figure Recalls Events Surrounding the Declaration of War

The late Ken Corbett, an heir to the local ironmongery and farm machinery manufacturing business S. Corbett & Son was born in the town, making him a true Wellingtonian. In his personal written account he records the details of the war's declaration, as imparted to the gathered populace in Market Square.

'The owner of the Wrekin Hotel, a Mrs Chinnock, commonly allowed the upstairs front room equipped with a vast bay window to be opened and used for local announcements and Election results and as such became a popular gathering point in the square.'

From the huge crowds gathered in Market Square that day, it can be assumed that the news represented far greater importance to the local populace than it did to *The Journal*, as can be gleaned from the contemporary photographs and brief captions accompanying the day's events (see illustration).

At this early euphoric stage of the war, Wellingtonians and the

The Journal: *declaration of war. [Caption reads: 'The crowds were gathered to await the arrival of the Territorials.']* **(The Journal** *edition – Saturday, 8 August 1914)*

country as a whole were in triumphal mood and looking forward to the confrontation with Germany, which would be settled quickly by England's 'brave fighting lads' at the front.

The Limited Media Available to Wellingtonians to Monitor the War's Progress

This great milestone in history did not pass unnoticed by even the most sceptical of Wellingtonians and it seemed that along with the whole

War awaited, as printed in **The Journal** *– 4 August 1914*

nation, their worst fears had now been realized. The spectre of war had been looming across Europe for many years and had now come to its deadly fruition. It seems incredible to us in the modern era that the people were so blasé about the intense fighting already taking place on Continental Europe during the opening weeks of the war.

It is worth noting that these spectacular world events occurred long before the advent of national broadcasts on radio and television and all the other media we now take for granted. There was no equivalent to the first-hand 'live' reports from specialist journalists on the war front that we expect today. All war news was, by definition, rendered second hand having been written first in notebooks by military observers, which would then be censored before being issued to the press via an official communiqué, or by the occasional visiting national newspaper correspondent (again officially censored) authorized to write daily or weekly reports.

It was then typed up, if there was time, before being posted or sent by telegraph if the news was urgent.

However, the average person on the streets of Wellington prior to the outbreak and certainly throughout most of the hostilities would have balked at the thought that they or any other UK citizens were ignorant or even poorly informed about local, national or world events. They would point out that thanks to the advent of the telegraph, telephone and steam train (all considered wonders of the age by spanning huge distances at speeds considered impossible only a few decades earlier) local and global news, current affairs and weather reports were brought to their kitchen tables every week, along with the milk, in the shape of the local weekly newspaper. In Wellington's case this service was provided by *The Wellington Journal and Shrewsbury News* – known locally as *The Journal* – a broadsheet publication established in 1850.

National daily newspapers were more the domain of the wealthy. As a consequence the average working man was perhaps less well informed with regards to indepth reporting of the war,. However, the newly implemented practice of syndication (sharing) in which provincial newspapers, such as *The Journal*, bought in stories from the larger newspapers, dubbed nationals, meant everyone had access to most current events.

Nationals could afford to send their own specially assigned correspondents along with the new breed of professional newsman called photojournalists, whose pictures brought a graphic and immediate feel to the events as they unfolded. Alongside the stills camera, a new toy called the film camera appeared and was quickly employed as a propaganda tool to influence public opinion and help garner war support back home. Hand-cranked with clockwork mechanisms, which were mounted on heavy wooden tripods, they could hardly be described as easily portable. Yet somehow they found their way onto many inaccessible battlefields and captured for the first time the fighting soldier in action.

Many big battles were actually restaged and filmed well after the

event to favour the side in charge of the camera, changing the outcome to make it look more successful than it was.

The full potential of the movie camera as a tool of state propaganda was to be perfected by the Nazis in the Second World War. It helped convince their nation of the legitimacy of their cause and enhanced Hitler's creed of personality and public image that he so carefully nurtured.

A movie cameraman in action on the Western Front circa 1916

The *Daily Mail* particularly was keen to bring graphic images to its readers and even produced collectible cigarette-style cards depicting many aspects of the fighting, focusing mainly on the Western Front in France.

The other communication marvel of the age – the ticker tape or telegraph machine – was instrumental in keeping the local citizens abreast of the latest war events. At the office of *The Journal* located in

Daily Mail *sample cigarette card*

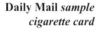

Church Street ticker tape streams were stuck to the inside of the window so that passersby could read the latest news events as they were being typed.

The British Expeditionary Force Pass Through Town to War

When war was declared, British towns witnessed a huge mobilisation of men and equipment pulled by the main haulage power: the horse. They were needed to transport various items such as munitions and vital supplies to keep a massive army functioning. They passed through towns en route to training and embarkation camps.

Manpower and the machinery of war passed through Wellington during the early weeks of the war in the shape of a unit from the Chester Brigade of the Royal Field Artillery (RFA) on its way to Northern France and the Western Front.

Their appearance brought the conflict that little bit closer home to Wellingtonians. It forced them to consider that perhaps there really was a war being fought by Britain, including many of their own townsfolk enlistees, just across the channel in Europe, a mere 100 miles away from the country's eastern coastline. The men and horses from the Territorial Army Yeomanry and other brigades passing through the town were quartered in the picture hall on Mill Bank, Constitution Hill School or the grounds of Wellington College.

Chester Brigade Royal Field Artillery passing through Wellington - **The Journal**

The Journal: *Horses in Wellington college grounds.*

Wellington indoor market hall and its Corn Exchange were commandeered by the Chester RFA Brigade as billets for their men and stabling for a limited number of horses

Chester brigade billeted at Wellington's market hall and Corn Exchange.

Wellington station today

Wellington Station and the Role of the National Railway in the War

Compared to the horse, the railway played a minor role in moving men and supplies across the country prior to departure for Europe and the Western Front. Horses were required at the front in ever increasing numbers and were caught in a bottleneck. This was due to a chronic shortage of adequate horse-adapted railway stock carriages. Inevitably this caused blockages at the remounting centres, which were becoming overcrowded. Although the rail system carried the men and their equipment to the coast for embarkation onto ferries, they could not take them directly to the battlefield once they'd reached France. This was because our rolling stock did not match the French system, so bulk items including soldiers had to travel by either lorry power or horsepower or else on foot.

Wellington station, which opened in 1848, was one of many national railway staions to be commandeered during the war and thus play an important role in transporting men across the UK to the ferry ports for embarkation to France and beyond.

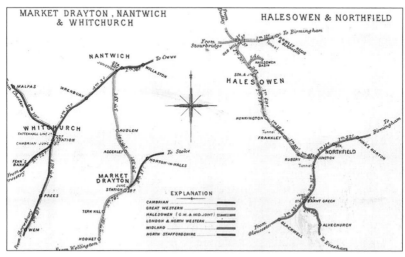

Wellington station line map circa 1914

Station platforms became the scene of mass departures of soldiers made all the more poignant as local people said heart-wrenching goodbyes to sons, brothers, husbands and lovers whom perhaps they

Railway platform soldier's goodbyes - concerned woman with child

would never see alive again. Judging from the expressions in some candid wartime snaps, many were pleased to go and do their bit for England and simply chose to ignore the concerns of their relatives.

Britain's railway system became subject to War Office control very early on in the war following the passing of the Defence of the Realm Act (DORA). Operators were also subject to fixed rate contracts, which meant they could not run at a cumulative profit for the duration of the war regardless of cost escalation. Consequently when the war ended the lack of investment and worn out rolling stock conspired to bankrupt several companies.

The General Mood of the Country, and in Wellington, at the Outbreak of War

The UK was no longer an isolated group of islands surrounded by seas controlled by the Royal Navy. For the second time in 100 years it was committed to fighting a war on mainland Europe to protect its own borders from possible invasion. This time it was fighting for national loyalty, a cause that the average man in the street understood and believed in. He felt the need to keep would-be foreign invaders at bay and to protect the sovereign, His Majesty King George V and his realm from German oppression.

Lord Kitchener's explicitly-worded recruitment posters screamed out to potential recruits in highly patriotic terms. It worked until some recalled that the British royal family was at the time dubbed the 'House of Hanover' due to its German heritage. This was changed discreetly to the very English

King George V (reign: 1910–1936)

Wellington outdoor market stall in Church Street – **The Journal**

sounding 'House of Windsor' and as the war's progression became that much bloodier and British casualties mounted, this gesture smoothed the tide of public opinion.

Wellington outdoor market street stalls on Church Green – **The Journal**

Wellington's Temporary Outdoor Market in 1914

The inconvenience of the commandeered indoor market hall prompted the ousted traders to re-introduce the Wellington open-air market. This comprised stalls that stretched the length of Church Street and covered the Church Green fronting All Saints Church.

The prolonged summer weather ensured a splendid turnout and brought back memories of the old times before the advent of the indoor market when traders sold their wares from stalls on the street.

The general mood of optimism in the town belied the gathering storm coming its way across the Channel from the Western Front and beyond.

War News as reported in *The Journal*

The following reports one and two are extracts drawn from the pages of *The Journal* covering the period from September to December 1914. Printed under the first left hand column of Page 6 headed *'THE WAR'*

Gallant British Stand in Northern France

The great battle upon the issue of which so much greatly depends is reported to be still in progress in northern France. The Germans with their vast forces have for several days been gradually pressing back the allied British and French towards Paris, though with terrible loss of life to the invaders themselves for every inch of ground gained. The French seat of government has been temporarily removed from Paris to Bordeaux. The Belgian cathedral city of Melines has suffered the same fate as its neighbour, Louvaine having been wantonly destroyed, together with many priceless art treasures, by modern German vandals. Our British troops have not fared so badly as was at first feared, official figures published this week showing a total of 10,345 men killed, wounded or missing since the commencement of hostilities, the 'missing' comprising an overwhelmingly large proportion of the whole.

Allies Position Strengthened in the Western theatre

It was officially reported on Saturday) the fighting was proceeding without an striking feature, but the Allies continued to strengthen their position in detail. They had captured various points of advantage north and south of Ypres and attacks north of Arras (by three German regiments) and south of Ypres had been beaten back. The weight of the enemy's artillery fire had decreased and, though the cannonade on Saturday was more active, the duel turned in favour of the defenders, who continued to use more powerful guns.

[5 December 1914]

Bold Beginnings

'The lamps are going out all over Europe and we shall not see them lit again in our lifetime.'

(Sir Edward Grey – the Foreign Secretary's fateful comments at news of the outbreak of war – 1914)

National Response to the War and Local Recruitment in Wellington

'Who would not fight for England –
who would not fling a life I'
the ring to meet a tyrant's rage.
And glory in the strife?'

(Source: Soldier's Farewell (cartoon and verse) –
The Journal - 15 August 1914)

The British Army in 1914 was weak in comparison to her Allies and other European armies including Germany's which had massive standing armies and could also call on many thousands of reservists. In the light of these facts it is surprising to note that for a European country supposedly at the heart of regional politics, Britain was not fully equipped to fulfill all treaty obligations. It was the least prepared for a war that had been a possibility for a number of years prior to the outbreak and had turned into a certainty within a very short space of time.

SHROPSHIRE ROYAL HORSE ARTILLERY.

Recruits are now wanted

FOR THE RESERVE UNIT

of the above Battery.

Men accustomed to horses preferred, age 19 to 35, pay and allowances as in Regular Army.

The obligation incurred is for

HOME SERVICE

with the option for signing for foreign service also.

Applications to be made to

THE RIDING SCHOOL,

COLEHAM, SHREWSBURY,

any day from 10 a.m. to 4 p.m.

God Save the King.

Notice of war service –
The Journal *August 1914.*

Kitchener poster - Your country needs you –
The Journal

Propaganda was rife in both national and local papers including *The Journal.* It carried a blatant call to arms aimed at young men and inferred it was unpatriotic not to respond in the light of the perceived threat to King and country.

The famous poster depicting Lord Kitchener was added to the recruitment campaign very early on in the war. It was presumed that Britain's most famous military figure would appeal to the patriotic zeal of the thousands of young men up and down the land who were anxious to enlist.

Other propaganda posters started to appear in public places that inveigled the younger menfolk (and those of service age – including family men) to regard military life in a new and intrepid light.

Industry was quick to jump on the bandwagon and promote products in a patriotic light, advertising anything from chocolate to cigarettes

Wartime propaganda poster -
Daddy, what did YOU do in the
war? Imperial War Museum

Example advert: advertising
cigarettes - **The Journal**

with cartoon depictions of dashing young men in Army uniform (usually arm in arm with a young woman).

Military-style lists informing all and sundry where to report and the contacts for various Yeomanry and KSLI battalions around the town and the local area were widely circulated and advertised in *The Journal*.

The Territorial and Reserve Forces Act of 1907 implemented by Richard Burdon Haldane, then Secretary of War resulted in the creation of Territorial Forces nationwide.

SHROPSHIRE   YEOMANRY.

"D," OR WELLINGTON SQUADRON.

The Head Quarters of the Regiment are at Kingston House, St. Alkmund's Square, Shrewsbury. "D" Squadron Head Quarters:—9, Bridge Road, Wellington.

The Officers in the Squadron are as follows:—Squadron Leader: Captain Cecil U. Corbet, Sundorne. 2nd Lieutenant G. C. Woolryche-Whitmore, Larden Grange, Much Wenlock; 2nd Lieutenant The Hon. H. C. Vane. Captain and Adjutant: J. E. D. Holland, 7th Dragoon Guards. Drill Instructor: Sergeant-Major H. C. Hounslow, 9, Bridge Road, Wellington, Salop.

The authorised strength of the Squadron is as follows:—Squadron Sergt.-Major, 1; Squadron Quartermaster-Sergeant, 1; Farrier Sergeant, 1; Sergeants, 5; Trumpeters, 2; Corporals, 6; Shoeing Smiths, 4; Saddler, 1; Privates, 89. Total 110.

Places, Days, and Times of Drill, from March until May:—Much Wenlock: Mondays, 6 p.m.; Newport: Tuesdays, 7 p.m.; Wellington: Thursdays, 7 p.m.; Shifnal: Fridays, 7 p.m.; Market Drayton, 4 p.m.; Bridgnorth: Saturdays, 2 p.m.

Eligible Young Men desirous of joining above Squadron, should apply to Sergt.-Major Hounslow, 9, Bridge Road, or at any Drill Station enumerated above

---

SHROPSHIRE ROYAL HORSE ARTILLERY

Headquarters—Shrewsbury

LEFT SECTION—HEAD QUARTERS: King Street, Wellington.

The Drill Hall was erected in 1889, and cost £900.

OFFICER COMMANDING:—Major R. A. Newill (A.).
Captain C. V. Bulstrode (A); Surgeon-Captain G. Mackie, M.B.;
Captain and Adjutant, E. E. Rich. Lieutenant R. D. Newill. Lieutenant J. H. Leake.
Drill Instructor: Sergt.-Major A. Shattock.

The Section comprises:—1 Staff; 1 Battery Sergeant-Major; 1 Battery Quartermaster Sergeant; 3 Sergeants; 2 Corporals; 4 Bombardiers; 2 Trumpeters; 1 Collar-maker; 1 Wheeler; 1 Shoeing Smith; 24 Gunners, 24 Drivers, and 7 Batmen. Total 72.

There is a Reading, Recreation, and Gymnasium Room in connection with the Drill Hall for the use of the Members of the Battery.

All information can be had from Sergeant-Major A. Shattock, at the Drill Hall.

"C" (WELLINGTON) COMPANY 4TH BATT. K.S.L.I.

ARMOURY AND DRILL ROOM—MARKET HALL BUILDINGS.

OFFICERS: Captain W. M. Huntbach; Lieutenant G. W. Huntbach; Lieutenant W. D. Howes Roberts; Lieutenant C. F. Leake. COL.-SERGT.-INSTRUCTOR: C. Hinde.

The Company comprises 4 Officers. 1 Colour-Sergeant-Instructor, 5 Sergeants, 4 Corporals, 109 Privates. Total 123. Right-half Company—Wellington; Left-Half Company—Market Drayton.

Class shooting at the Wrekin Range, every Saturday, at 2 p.m., from 1st March, until 15th October. There is a Recreation Room in connection with the Company, open every evening from 7 to 9 p.m., except Saturdays, Sundays, and Mondays.
For Drill, see Notice Board, Market Hall.

All information can be had from Col. Sergt.-Instructor C. Hinde, at the Barracks, Market Buildings.

Wellington company lists – **The Journal**

SHROPSHIRE ROYAL HORSE ARTILLERY.

LEFT SECTION—HEADQUARTERS : King Street, Wellington

Officers—Major R. A. Newill, T. D., Captain and Adjutant E. E. Rich, R,H.A., Captain Surgeon G. Mackie, M.B., Lieut. R. D. Newill, Lieut. H. J. Leake, Drill Instructor, Sergeant-Major Shattock, R.H.A.,King Street.

The Section comprises 2 Officers, 1 Staff, 1 Battery-Sergeant Major, 1 Battery-Quartermaster-Sergeant. 3 Sergeants, 2 Corporals, 4 Bombardiers, 1 Trumpeter, 1 Shoeing-Smith, 1 Collar-maker, 1 Wheeler, 25 Gunners and 27 Drivers. Total 70.

A large room has been added to the Drill Hall for the benefit of the Members of the Battery and is used for lectures, etc. The members also by payment of a small subscription have an assortment of daily and weekly papers and various games.   There is also a Gymnasium in connection with the Battery. All information can be had from Sergeant-Major A. Shattock at the Drill Hall.

"C" (WELLINGTON & MARKET DRAYTON) CO'Y.
4TH BATT. KING'S SHROPSHIRE LIGHT INFANTRY.

HEADQUARTERS—Wellington

Armoury and Drill Room : Market Hall Buildings. Officers : Captain W. M. Huntbach : Lieutenants G. W. Huntbach, W. D. H. Roberts and C. F. Leake ; Sergeant-Instructor Davey.

The Company comprises 1 Captain, 3 Lieutenants. 1 Sergeant-Instructor, 6 Sergeants, 4 Corporals, 139 Privates.   There are 2 Machine Guns.

Drill every Tuesday and Wednesday at 7-30 o'clock. Class-firing at the Wrekin Range every Saturday at 2 p.m. from 1st March, until 15th October.

The Reading and Recreation Room is open during the winter.

"D" (WELLINGTON) SQUADRON SHROPSHIRE YEOMANRY.

HEADQUARTERS OF SQUADRON :—9 Bridge Road. The Officers attached to " D " Squadron are as follows :—Adjutant, Captain J. E. D. Holland, 7th (Princess Royal) Dragoon Guards ; Officer Commanding Squadron, Captain C. U. Corbett ; Second-Lieutenant G. C. Wolryche-Whitmore, Second-Lieut. P. E. Frank ; Drill Instructor, Squadron-Sergeant-Major H. C. Hounslow.

The following comprises a Squadron of Yeomanry :—1 Squadron-Sergeant-Major, 1 Quartermaster-Sergeant, 1 Farrier-Sergeant,5 Sergeants, 2 Trumpeters, 6 Corporals, 4 Shoeing Smiths, 1 Saddler, 85 Privates. Total : Rank and File, 96 ; All Ranks, 111.

Preliminary Drills take place from March to May. Annual Training, usually in May. Musketry from March to September.

Notification of Territorial Army drills and training schedules

Edgbaston house - recruitment office with crowd of volunteers in 1914

*Kitchener recruitment advert - **The Journal.** Volunteers enlisted at the main centre based at Edgbaston House on Walker Street as well as at the former YMCA building.*

The Act sought to reorganize the country's former domestic defence forces comprising the Volunteer Army, county militia and Yeomanry Brigades and combine them into one force.

This was to be managed on a county by county basis with each regiment or battalion allocated a Regular Army officer to oversee them and offer advice.

Volunteers serving as territorials meant they were never compelled to serve abroad. However the generals and the grassroots rank and file volunteered for active service abroad so were inducted into the British Expeditionary Force (BEF) regiments and saw action all over the world.

Wellington's own territorial battalions, comprising

Edgbaston House - present day

Shropshire Yeomanry, Shropshire Royal Horse Artillery and a battalion of the KSLI were mobilised accordingly.

Townsfolk witnessed their movements as they joined the rapidly-growing BEF that would pass through Wellington en route to regimental barracks or training camps across the country prior to embarkation to France and other theatres of war.

At the beginning of the war, recruitment was brisk in Wellington. *The Journal* in common with most national and regional newspapers ran the famous Kitchener volunteer recruitment advert from late August 1914 until the end of the year.

The YMCA building at the top of Crown Street, which saw so many men sign up, would later be adapted partly for use as a convalescent hospital.

The youth of the day in Wellington and across the nation, saw enlistment as a chance to escape their humdrum everyday lives for a few months and enjoy a brief adventure in the company of friends before returning home unscathed having served King and country.

It was a chance to see a little bit of the world and then return as a man having won their spurs in battle. For others of lesser repute it was a foolproof means of escaping the law. Enlistment was viewed as a means to an end: a safe refuge in the ranks to hide out in plain sight until the heat had died down.

The grim reality was somewhat different. As the KSLI was the main recruiter, the names of its slaughtered rank and file would eventually adorn many a war memorial in Wellington and indeed across the whole of Shropshire. This regiment's overall sacrifice is commemorated in their own shrine at the National Memorial Arboretum, Alrewas in Staffordshire.

Alrewas National Memorial Arboretum KSLI monument.

Fodder for the Guns (Part 1):
Wellingtonians' Great War stories

This is the first of the stories told to me by various Wellington families about their relatives who served. Wellingtonian George Evans (now in his nineties) a retired teacher, author and local historian describes his father Eric's participation as a serving soldier, one of Kitchener's Volunteer Army, in the Great War and the bitter recriminations that followed his service after becoming a repatriated casualty who quickly joined the swelling ranks of the forgotten.

George Evans - local author

'*My father Eric was born in 1892 in a little hamlet called Weston-under-Redcastle about fifteen miles to the north west of Wellington and lived with his father and brothers.*

As their family business was cattle farming they regularly took stock into Wellington Livestock Market and so he came to know and love the town.

In 1914 aged 22, and answering the call for volunteers for the war, he said goodbye to family, took his horse called Tom and rode to Prees Heath where the Shropshire Yeomanry had a training camp.and recruitment centre As it was principally a cavalry regiment he promptly volunteered himself and Tom.

I never asked dad if Tom was consulted about joining up but nevertheless they both found that they had taken the King's shilling [slang for Army enlistment].

Eric Evans in uniform

He later admitted to me that he was motivated by romantic notions of heroic adventure for the conflict ahead, much the same as many other young men in those early, heady days of the war.

At the time of his enlistment Dad had been living in lodgings in Victoria Avenue in Wellington and fancied the landlady's daughter Mabel Fail.

She was a sweet-natured, attractive young girl of eighteen summers who was destined to be my mother.

However, they were to be parted for the time being as Father was whisked away with the regimental inductees to the Curragh their remount centre [now famed as a horse racing complex], near Dublin, Ireland for intensive cavalry training.

'Once arrived they found themselves in the the world of cavalry professionals, which was dominated by the regimental sergeant major who was to train them to ride cavalry style – hard and fast. His gruff parade ground manner soon sorted the men from the boys. When dealing with new recruits he always used horses well trained to understand certain key words of command.

"Mount" was the first and so the nervous riders took to the saddle.

"Walk march" was the next order. This prompted the horses to move forward at a steady pace.

Mabel Fail - mother of George Evans

"Canter" was the next. The horses changed pace automatically to the verbal command.

"Gallop" was the next command. The horses adapted easily but the riders struggled.

"Charge" was the final bellowed command. Off went the horses at top speed with their reluctant riders going around in a circle.

"Halt" was the sudden instruction – instantly obeyed by the horses but not the riders.

This resulted in an untidy heap of red-faced soldiers sprawling on the ground.

The sergeant major stared first then berated his trainees with a query issued at the top of his voice: "Who told you to dismount?" After this perilous introduction to cavalry training Dad was posted to Egypt – or rather 'egg-wiped' as he disdainfully liked to pronounce it.

Egypt at the time was a British protectorate, meaning satellite or sphere of influence but not a full bona fide colony. As they had certain vital interests in the country – not least the Suez shipping canal – to protect and defend, troops were duly dispatched to ward off a threatened attack from the Ottoman Empire-ruling Turkey.

Their first engagement was indeed to be against forces of the Ottoman Empire of Turkey who had come into the war on the side of Germany – threatening all British interests around the Mediterranean.

They were making their presence felt in the Middle East by attacking Britain's colonies and protectorates, such as Egypt, wherever and whenever they could.

Whilst preparing for their first full-blown cavalry charge the generals suddenly decided against this strategy. This was as early as 1915 and news of other cavalry defeats were now filtering through from the Western Front.

Consequently, dear old Dad's regiment was immediately disbanded and the whole contingent of Shropshire Yeomanry was transferred to the KSLI, 4th Battalion.

Dad was not best pleased and called them 'the King's silly little idiots' instead.

Following a series of regular duty rotations he experienced many trench-based engagements and also many incidents considered to be on the funny side of trench life.

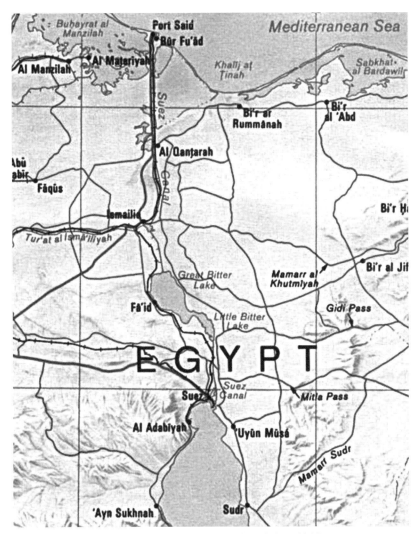

Map of Egypt and the Suez Canal circa 1914

On one occasion he leapt into a trench, which had been recently vacated by the Allied Portuguese Army. As he jumped in, a mud-covered object caught his eye which turned out to be a discarded tobacco pipe. He diligently cleaned it and on examining it closely the maker's name revealed itself to be Pelican and Snelson of Shrewsbury.

He kept it and smoked it all through the remainder of the war up until he was discharged.

In 1917 he found himself trenchbound again and fighting at the infamous Ypres in Belgium.

Although this was well after the main campaigns, the region was still a hotspot for further fighting They were stationed in some trenches that were very close to the Germans.

In one engagement the order to attack came and Dad had his rifle in one hand and a Mills Bomb [hand grenade] in the other. By now he had attained the rank of corporal and was heroically leading his men over the top. A German sniper in the opposite trench took aim and hit the hand holding the bomb shooting the top off his left thumb.

Fearing the bomb would explode, Dad threw it as far as he could towards the enemy trenches before ducking down and seeing to his wound.

After applying a field dressing from the kit every infantryman carried, he continued the attack and was crossing no-man's land when another German bullet found its way into his left leg, passing through the shinbone. He dived into a trench and found a dead soldier and took the deceased's field dressing to use on his leg. Through a combination of dressing and binding of the wound using his uniform's putties [long winding tapes of cloth used on the lower legs as part of the uniform] he stabilised the injury and waited a day and part of a night until his own company's stretcher bearers found him and brought him back through the lines for proper treatment. On examination at a triage centre his was considered a 'blighty wound' meaning discharge and transportation back to England.

Once home he found himself in a Cambridge military hospital, which turned out to be very fortunate for Dad. The chief surgeon decided to patch up his leg wound rather than amputate – which was common practice at the time.

The leg healed well but he was left with some impairment that affected his walking.

He was later to throw away his First World War campaign medals in disgust after a bitter row over the meagre Army pensions awarded to veterans.

When he spoke to me about his experiences he said he thought the war was stupid.

He was very scathing about the way the "idiot generals" managed things and he subscribed to the idea that they were lions led by donkeys [a phrase popular in the day]

He later became a first lieutenant in the Home Guard in the Second World War doing his bit again for King and country in another "stupid war" as he called it, which was started by a certain Mr Hitler.

George's mother met and married Eric in Wellington after his return from the Great War but the lead up to their happy union is worth telling due to its relevance to the war and the wider conflict.

In 1914, Mother was a dressmaker and had her own business with her sister in King Street in Wellington. Her sister decided to end their partnership but luckily for Mother she was making dresses for Orleton Hall, home of a Mrs Trefewsis, one of the ladies-in-waiting for Lord Forester. Mrs Trefewsis' husband was appointed aide-de-camp to the Jamaican governor, who as it turned out was dictatorial for a diplomat supposedly skilled in diplomacy.

Mother was invited to go to Jamaica with Mrs Trefewsis, as part of her entourage, to make dresses exclusively for her at Government House in Kingston the capital city.

She had complete access to the governor's residence King's House and she loved to sit in his throne-like chair, when it was available. She made dresses and hats for the ladies who lived there.

Whenever a British ship sailed into Kingston Harbour the governor insisted imperiously that he would meet it. The official state car was bought out every single time replete with police motorbike outriders. All traffic across the town of Kingston would be halted to allow the convoy to pass unhindered.

In 1917 Mum received a letter to say her mother was dangerously ill and could she please come home immediately. She booked passage to England on the first available boat, which was a Fyffes banana boat, a merchantman with very few passengers. They laid on special food for her at the captain's table, which included jugged hare made with an alcohol-free recipe as she was teetotal at the time. They were having dinner at the captain's table one night when suddenly there was a very loud bang which turned out to be a torpedo exploding. The captain leapt up and shouted: "My God, we're hit".

Somebody rushed in and informed him the ship was sinking so the captain gave the order to abandon ship.

All lifeboats were successfully launched and consequently no one was lost.

Having pulled away from the ship as it went down, the submarine surfaced alongside Mum's lifeboat. They were closely scrutinised by the German U-boat commander who decided they were all civilians and non-military and spared them from further harassment.

The captain ordered them to keep rowing in the direction of Ireland some 300 miles away.

During their perilous voyage he turned to Mother and said: "Sing us a hymn, Miss Fail, to keep up morale." She did and they all joined in.

They were picked up by an Allied Q-boat, which were disguised to look like merchant ships but were actually submarine hunters.

They were treated with great courtesy and landed in Ireland from where she made her way home to Wellington to help tend to her ailing mother.

Mum and Dad had been engaged since 1914 so in 1920 they married and in 1923 I came along.'

We shall hear more from this venerable old Wellingtonian, George Evans, later.

The next story about Wellington servicemen concerns an altogether more disparate local family and was told to me by Janet Eatough who is nearly 80 and still resides in the town. She told me about her relative, Private 7456 Thomas Chidley Osbourne from the 2nd Battalion, South Staffordshire Regiment (2/Staffs) who fought and died in the war as an infantryman on the Western Front on 1 February 1915. He was born in Birmingham, enlisted in Lichfield and resident in Ashton and his family was resident in Wellington during and after the Great War.

My paternal great uncle Thomas died in France in February 1915.

He was killed just three weeks after he had joined up and gone to war. He was 35-years-old and had volunteered like so many other young men. As a result of his death his three older brothers also enlisted; one of them was my grandfather William. Two years later my father Leonard Osbourne joined up at just 17-years-old.

I never knew my great uncle personally as I was born twenty years after his death. My father never spoke of him and none of the family knew anything about him either. My father, who was born in Eastbourne, was left in Birmingham with his grandmother at two years of age. The rest of the family settled in Wellington and had two more children. My father stayed with his grandmother right up until he enlisted and then joined William and his family in 1919 after the war ended.

Thomas was only 9-months-old when his father died aged just 29, leaving four sons. His mother remarried and he lived with her up to the time of his enlistment and subsequent death. For fifteen years he shared close

Private TC Osbourne 2/Staffs – killed in action 01/02/15

family life with his nephew (my father) so they must have loved and cared for one another very much.

He left a great gap in the family when he died. His mother received his service medal and kept it until she passed it on to his uncle Arthur who left it to his grandson who took great care of it. 'I only found out about Thomas because I wanted to find out about my family tree. I feel I have come to know him very well. I think about him a lot and because my father knew him more as an older brother than an uncle it brings him closer to me. It makes him almost a part of me. I'm nearly 80 and the oldest of the Osbourne family and have no one to talk to about Thomas. The Great War denied a lot of young men and women the chance to marry and have children.

I feel as sorry for Thomas as I do for myself and the countless families who were denied a chance to know their relatives and love them.

Thomas may be gone from our lives but he is not forgotten.

Other documentary evidence supplied by Mrs Eatough helps us to fill in the gaps of Thomas's war service and how he may have met his death. The following extract is taken from: *A History of the South Staffs Regiment* by J.P. Jones.

The Battalion departed Southampton docks 2pm Tuesday, 11 August 1914, on a ship called the 'Irrawady' and docked at Le Havre on Thursday 13 August.

For the whole of the year 1915 the Battalion were operating in the La Bassee sector. They then moved into the line at Le Touret on 2 January taking over from the 2nd Grenadier Guards.

The trenches were indescribable, almost waist deep in water in many places. Under these conditions daily relief was a necessity and the companies interchanged daily. Two days in trenches and two days in billets was the order. During the month of January sickness in the Battalion was rather heavy. Two officers and 96 men going sick, nearly all suffering from severe cold, rheumatism and swollen feet. The marvel is that the list was not greater owing to the privations endured. The filth and dirt of the trenches transformed the usually smart men into dirty scarecrows. But it was difficult for men burrowing in the ground to preserve anything like an aspect of cleanliness. Fortunately baths and washhouses had been installed in the rest areas and the men were able to wash themselves, shave and get their hair cut. There was a recurrence of fighting on the 25 and 26 of January to mark the celebration of the German Emperor's birthday. About 6 am on the morning of 26 January a German deserter came in and warned our men that there would be an attack in half an hour. Punctually to the moment came the attack, the trenches in the salient were blown in at once and the line was broken. The 2nd Division was ordered to concentrate on the main road through Mesplaux and await orders. They were not called upon until 28, as a counter attack had driven the Germans far enough back to restore the somewhat broken line and strengthen it. The 2nd South Staffs taking over from the 1st Kings Royal Rifles in the trenches in Rue De Bois. 'A' and 'B' Companies in the line with 'C' and 'D' Companies in reserve billets.

On the last day of January Lt Col C. S. Davidson C.B. was admitted to hospital and subsequently returned to England. The command of the 2nd Battalion was taken over by Lt.-Col P.C.L. Routledge and on 3rd February the 2nd Battalion SS went to Givenchy to relieve the Munster Fusiliers and half the Gloucester Regiment.

The Germans were continually attacking but making little headway being driven out of positions they had captured by our repeated counter-attacks. The system of holding the line was now altered, two Battalions being placed in the line in each section, each finding their own supports the usual method being to put two companies in the front line and two in reserve. Companies relieving each other alternately every forty-eight hours.

Brief History of the King's Shropshire Light Infantry up to the Great War

The predecessors of what became the King's Shropshire Light Infantry (KSLI) Regiment can trace their history back to 1755 when it was decided to augment the strength of the national Regular Army by raising ten brand new regiments of foot from across Britain.

Much like the period leading up to the First World War, the middle to late eighteenth century was an era of unrest and potential threat from yet another European power – in this case France.

This came at a similar time of rapid expansion in British foreign power and influence brought about through trade and colonisation of new territories such as the New World – the name given to the Americas and in particular Canada and North America. Once again Britain was backed by a mighty navy and great financial wealth.

France was regarded by Britain as just another would-be colonial power with interests abroad, actively instigating wars to exert its presence and extend its own influence. Much the same as Germany aspired to do across the world and in particular in the UK's colonies in the run up to the Great War.

And so in the beginning, a letter of appointment went to Colonel William Whitmore of Apley near Bridgnorth, with the instruction to raise a regiment from the county of Shropshire.

Being a beautiful rural county, it was argued that the recruited peasantry would fight more vehemently for the right to maintain its integrity unmolested by foreign invasion. This group was referred to as 'the backbone of the Army' – a colourful metaphor that would be added to every recruiting sergeant's patter across the land and was guaranteed to swell the breast of many a proud young man and hopefully stimulate their desire to sign up.

Armed with local knowledge, Whitmore recruited mainly from the famous local trowmen or barge haulers based along that mighty artery of trade at the time, the River Severn and a trade known to be affected by periodic fluctuations in pay.

This was hard manual work demanding exceptional physical strength and stamina fuelled by an overly enthusiastic thirst for local ales, as many a riverside inn would testify.

General William Whitmore, founder of the KSLI Regiment

With frequent downtime and seasonal lapses of income the promise of regular army pay would have appealed greatly to these hardy trowmen, especially those with wives and children. These new regiments of foot were to be raised to defend British colonial interests nearer to home too, particularly as the French were making other inroads across Europe. The wider general mobilisation was also to protect expanding British interests in the Mediterranean area: specifically the newly acquired deep water ports and naval bases such as Gibraltar, Malta and Alexandria. Whitmore established the new regiment's first headquarters in Bridgnorth as a centre for training and recruitment. He'd insisted it was situated in a bustling centre for trade and administration and be near enough to the family seat at Apley.

The town had long been associated with the military. It had served first as a Cavalier stronghold complete with ancient castle and later as a Roundhead when it surrendered after a lengthy siege in the English Civil War (only to be systematically destroyed by Oliver Cromwell's men as punishment for non-capitulation).

However not long after the formation of Whitmore's Regiment, (it was common practice in the eighteenth century to refer to regiments by their founder) their services were used as an emergency contingent in a different European-based theatre called the Seven Years War. As a consequence the embryonic KSLI found themselves stationed in Gibraltar from 1757 to 1763. The 57th Light Infantry of foot was converted to the 53rd Light Infantry and evolved into elements of the 83rd and 85th regiments.

The recognisable First World War regiment of the KSLI was reorganized in 1881 under the Childers Reforms of the British Army. This major shakeup of the armed forces was named after Sir Hugh Childers, Secretary of State for the Army at that time.

Under his reforms the regiment became an amalgamation of the 83rd (Shropshire) Regiment of Foot and the 85th (King's Light Infantry) Regiment of Foot which later became the 1st and 2nd Regular Battalions (1&2/Regulars). In March 1882 it was renamed The King's Shropshire Light Infantry.

The reforms also redesignated the militia and volunteer units within the regimental district as battalions of the regiment. The Shropshire and Royal Herefordshire militias

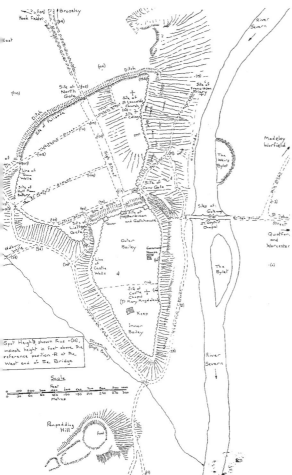

Map of Bridgnorth circa 1750

The Articles of Surrender
Of BRIDGNORTH CASTLE

I. That all Commissioned Officers of horse, and all Captains of Foot, shall march away to any of His Majesty's Garrison or Armies within 40 miles, with their horses and arms for themselves, and each of them to have a servant with his horse and sword, and wearing Apparel. Free quarter for 30 miles, and safe conduct, and not to march less than 8 miles a day.

II. That all inferior Commisioned Officers shall have liberty to march with their swords, and all the common Soldiers without Arms, to any of his Majesty's Garrisons or Armies within 40 miles as before stated, or laying down their arms, to live at their own habitations for a fortnight, and afterwards to take the negative Oath if they live within the County, or letters from hence to the Committees of the several Counties, where they intend to reside, and to have passes granted accordingly.

III. That all Clergymen, Townsmen, and Countrymen, within the castle, may have liberty to repair to their own habitations, provided they lay down their Arms, and a fortnight's time allowed them for taking the negative Oath, and not to live within a mile of the Parliament Garrisons; or otherwise if they should desire it, to march to any of the King's Garrisons or Armies.

IV. That all the wounded and sick persons in the castle, shall have liberty to reside in the Low Town, or elsewhere, till they be fit to travel, and then to have passes to go home or to any of the King's Garrisons or Armies.

V. That Sir Robert Howard, Sir Vincent Corbet, Sir Edward Acton, and Sir Francis Ottley, with each of them their horses and Arms, and two men apiece, with their horses and Swords and their masters wearing Apparel, shall have liberty to march to their several habitations, and to continue there for the space of two months in which time they are to make their election whether they will go to make their peace with Parliament, or go beyond Sea or to any of the King's Garrisons or Armies, and to have passes accordingly; they engaging themselves to do nothing prejudicial to the Parliament in the meantime.

VI. That Mr. Howard, Mr. Fisher and Mr. Grovenor, shall march away with their Horses and Arms, with one man apiece, with their Apparel and Swords, to any place within 40 miles.

VII. The Lieutenant Colonel Hosier and Doctor Lewen shall march away without horse or Arms, to any of the King's Garrisons, or any other place within 30 miles, provided it be not within this County.

VIII. That Mr. Milward, Captain of the Garrison, may have liberty to go with a horse to his house at Leighton, in this County, and to take with him his manuscripts, and their to live, taking the negative Oath within one month's, time, or is to march away out of the County with the rest.

IX. That the Clerks to the Commisioners, may have liberty to march as the rest of the inferior Officers, and to have the same conditions, and to take with them all papers concerning the Garrison, and their wearing Apparel.

X. That Lady Ottley, her children, and Maid servant, have liberty with their wearing Cloathes, to go to Pitchford, or the Hay, and there to live unmolested.

XI. That all women and Children within the castle, may have liberty to go to their own or any of their friends houses, provided it not be within a mile of this Garrison.

XII. That all Gentlemen, Officers, and Soldiers within the Castle, Strangers as well as others desiring to go beyond the sea, shall have passes accordingly, and letters to the Committees of their several Counties, to afford them the like conditions as to the Gentlemen of this County, upon the surrender of this Castle here granted.

XIII. That the Surgeon belonging to this Garrison, shall march away; and to have the same conditions as the inferior officers.

XIV. That the Gunners and Powdermen, with their mates, may march away as the rest of the Common Soldiers.

XV. That no violence, injury, or incivility, shall be offered to any who shall march out of this castle, must be protected in all things according to the tenor of these Articles, and that sufficient Hostages on both sides be given for the performance of all, and every, the matters here agreed upon.

XVI. That the Governor, and the rest of the Officers, shall do their utmost endeavors to prevent and preserve all the Ordinances, Arms, Ammunition, Victuals, Provisions, Goods, Bedding and all other Accommodations necessary and belonging to the castle other than what is allowed to be taken by the afforsaid articles, and all these safe and unspoiled, to be delivered up together with the Castle unto the Committee whom they shall appoint, and the Articles to be confirmed by the Governor.

XVII. That if these Articles be consented to, the Castle be surrendered by Seven of the clock tomorrow morning, and those who intend to march to Worcester, to quarter in the Low Town, or any other Town within 5 miles of the Garrison, upon the return of the trumpeter and Officer sent to Worcester, provided they come within two days.

XVIII. That if any officer, or Soldier shall in any way maliciously spoil his horse or Arms, or misdemean himself in his march, such misdemeanor shall not be extended further than upon the party offending, and upon they, justice shall be done according to the discipline of War.

XIX. That all Commisioned Officers certified by the Governor of the Castle, and upon his certificate be allowed to march accordingly; and that all troopers march away with their swords.

XX. That Mr. Edward Lathun be delivered to the mercy of Parliament.

The articles of surrender were signed in St. Mary Magdelene's Church on Sunday 26th April, 1646.
Sir Robert Howard, Sir Vincent Corbet, Sir Edward Acton and Sir Francis Ottley signed as Commisioners for the King.
Colonel Andrew Lloyd, Colonel Robert Clive and Robert Charleton signed as Commisioners for the Parliament.

Text copy of Bridgnorth castle surrender document

became the 3rd and 4th (Militia) Battalions; the 1st and 2nd Shropshire Rifle Volunteer Corps became the 1st and 2nd (Volunteer) Battalions (1&2/Volunteers) and the 1st Herefordshire (Herefordshire and Radnorshire) Rifle Volunteer Corps became affiliated as a volunteer battalion, but without change of name. As a result of the Haldane reforms of 1908, 1&2/Volunteers were merged to form the 4th Territorial Force (4/Territorials) and the two militia battalions were also merged to form the 3rd (Special Reserve) Battalion(3/Reserves). For the majority of the Shropshire volunteers enlisting for the Great War the KSLI was the regiment of choice. Both 1&2/Regulars established their headquarters at Copthorne Barracks Shrewsbury.

Sir Hugh Childers - Secretary of State 1881

Although they were billeted together in the same barracks they never actually met (except for two occasions in their recent history). The rotation of service was designed so that whilst one was on domestic or territorial duties the other was stationed abroad. *(*Copthorne Barracks is still there today but alas it is hosting other elements of the modern British Army. Its future as an Army facility seems in some doubt).

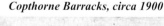

Copthorne Barracks, circa 1900

Copthorne Barracks – present day

Further foreign campaigns lay ahead as the battalions saw action in such far flung places as east Sudan in North Africa under Generals Gordon and Kitchener (later to head the army during the First World War). Their battles with the Mahdi's fanatical Islamist uprising centred around Khartoum, a British Fortress and base where Gordon was to meet his death and which was heroically recaptured by Lord Kitchener. The KSLI also fought in the Transvaal (South Africa) against the Boers, settlers of Dutch extraction who declared unilateral independence from British colonial rule. This was to be a long and bloody guerrilla war lasting from 1899 to 1902.

The Territorial Act of 1908 allowed for the formation of such units and under which the Shropshire Territorials were formed. It was intended that these regiments would be raised for domestic service and were never be expected to serve overseas.

As it transpired, these units, invariably to a man, volunteered for foreign service and were deployed on the Western Front as well as in the Middle East. As war approached most regiments of the British Army expanded to form new war service battalions and the KSLI was no exception. This was to accommodate the anticipated swelling of numbers as a result of the Kitchener enlistment campaign.

At the time of the First World War, elements of the Shropshire and Cheshire Territorials found themselves volunteered for service in France. These elements were merged with the KSLI battalions and so the new regiment embarked for France in 1914 as part of the First Army Division British Expeditionary Force (BEF) where it served on the Western Front through to 1918.

Recruiting advert for Territorials – as reprinted in **The Journal**

Basically they were the trench fodder facing the might of the well-trained, battle hardened and heavily-armed German *Kaiserheer*.

Notwithstanding, the Germans suffered heavy casualties and were reported to have complained bitterly about the intense and accurate machine gun fire they encountered from the British lines. This was despite the fact the BEF and the KSLI in particular were acutely short of heavier armaments on the Western Front, in particular machine guns.

German soldier Kaiserheer - Regular Army

The only concentrated fire they could muster was from their standard British Army issue bolt-action Lee-Enfield .303 rifles. As part of an inductee's rigorous training, volley fire and target practice produced riflemen of an exceptional standard. Their meticulous training produced the rapid withering volley fire frequently reported by the German infantrymen. Shooting competitions were organized on a regular basis and battalion teams were encouraged for many years prior to the war to encourage friendly rivalry within the regiment with cups awarded as prizes. This was to promote and encourage marksmanship thus producing a centre of excellence within the British Infantry. After distinguished service and many battle honours won in the First World War, including a Victoria Cross (VC), the KSLI went on to win many further battle honours in the Second World War including a further two VCs.

KSLI Battalions in the Great War
(Battle Honours and Medal Awards)

At the time of the Great War the regiment was increased to twelve battalions in total strength (with eight serving in in foreign theatres). The details are as follows:

The 1st Battalion

This was a pre-established regular battalion, based in the UK and Ireland 1903-14. Stationed in Tipperary in August 1914 it was mobilised for war and joined 16 Brigade, 6th Division, disembarking at St Nazaire, France, on 10 September. Participating in the early battles of the Aisne and Marne it served exclusively on the Western Front supporting many major campaigns.

Service Engagements of 1st Battalion on the Western Front to 1918

Fought in the First Battle of Ypres in 1914 and in the Ypres Salient of 1915, when it played a leading part in the attack on the Hooge positions in August. During April 1916, it was again at Ypres and took part in heavy fighting for the capture of positions on the Ypres-Langemarck road, losing their commanding officer, Lieutenant Colonel Luard who was killed in action there. It then saw service on the Somme in 1916 under Lieutenant Colonel Murray (Morval and Transloy Ridges; breaking of the Quadrilateral at Ginchy during the Battle of Flers-Courcelettes) and at Arras and Cambrai in 1917.

In January 1918, 1st Battalion was serving with Fifth Army and on 21 March it faced the final German Spring Offensive and was almost annihilated at Lagnicourt. Not one officer was left alive and only 53 other ranks survived this action.

The battalion was completely reformed under Lieutenant Colonel Meynell within ten days of being virtually destroyed. It rejoined the line at Ypres where it fought continuously in the Salient until late August.

After taking part in the fighting on the Hindenburg Line in 1918 with Fourth Army, including the heavy warfare around St Quentin, it served through the final operations against the Germans right up until the armistice in November.

Then 1/KSLI became part of the Rhineland occupation force (a demilitarized zone placed on Germany's Rhine border as part of the Versailles Treaty terms in 1919).

Total complement lost: 53 officers and 986 other ranks killed in action.

Battle Honours of 1st Battalion

France and Flanders 1914; France and Flanders 1915; France and Flanders 1916; France and Flanders 1917; France and Flanders 1918; Aisne 1914; Armentieres 1914; Hooge 1915; Somme 1916; Flers-Courcelette; Morval; Le Transloy; Hill 70; Cambrai 1917; Somme 1918; Hindenburg Line; Epehy; Cambrai 1918; Selle. (19 in total)

The 2nd Battalion

Another regular battalion, stationed in India 1903-14 and at Secunderabad in August 1914 when mobilised for war. It joined 80 Brigade, 27th Division and landed at Le Havre, France, on 21 December 1914 under Lieutenant Colonel Bridgford.

Service Engagements of 2nd Battalion to 1918

After some of the hardest fighting in the Ypres Salient at St Eloi and St Julien and on Frezenberg Ridge in the Second Battle of Ypres in the spring of 1915, 2nd Battalion moved to the relatively quiet sector (prior to July 1916) of the Somme.

It was sent to Salonika in December 1915 and spent nearly three years fighting the Bulgarians in Macedonia, based for the most part on the Struma front. From June 1916 to December 1917 2/KSLI was in trenches at Neohari and in the final offensive against Bulgaria, it was one of the first Allied units to entry enemy territory.

In November 1918, 2/KSLI absorbed the war-raised 8th Battalion and returned home via southern Turkey, after service at Batum on the Black Sea between December 1918 and June 1919, protecting oil supplies in the face of the Russian Civil War.

It was sent to Ireland, to Fermoy and Dublin during the last stages of British rule and was the last British battalion to leave Dublin Castle on the formation of the Irish Free State in 1921.

Battle Honours of 2nd Battalion

France and Flanders 1915; Macedonia 1915-18; Gravenstafel; Ypres 1915; St Julien Frezenberg; Bellewaerde. (seven).

The 3rd (Special Reserve) Battalion (formerly the old county militia, renamed in the 1908 reforms) served only as a training battalion during the war, with no overseas war service.

Served in Wales and Scotland until December 1917 when it moved to Cork and ended the war at Fermoy, later being formally absorbed into 2/KSLI. As a training battalion, it fed large numbers of men into the KSLI and other units.

The 4th Battalion (Territorials)

Mobilised for war on 5 August 1914, it was later expanded by the establishment of 2nd and 3rd line battalions.

The 1-4th Battalion

Originally formed from the county Rifle Volunteers (which became the two Volunteer Battalions of the KSLI), they were designated 4/Territorials in 1908 following the creation of the Territorial Force.

The 1-4th Battalion was mobilised at Shrewsbury on 4 August 1914 and embarked for India in October 1914. Its prime function, as with many of the Territorial battalions at this stage, was to take over routine imperial garrison duty, to free regular soldiers for active campaigning.

Service Engagements of 1-4th Battalion to 1918

It served in the Far East in Hong Kong, the Andaman Islands, Singapore and Rangoon 1914-17. Men of 1-4/KSLI escorted the prisoners of the German ship *Emden* to Australia after its battle with the Australian warship *Sydney* and later helped suppress the Singapore Mutiny by an Indian garrison battalion in 1915.

When it was en route to the UK, it spent time training in Ceylon as well as South Africa between May and June 1917, where it suffered greatly from sickness. The men never were able to visit home, despite a three-year absence, as in July 1917, 1-4/KSLI went straight from South Africa to the Western Front, attached to 63 Brigade (Royal Naval) Division around Arras.

Later that year, it moved to the Ypres Salient to take part in the great Passchendaele Offensive (Third Battle of Ypres) and suffered 130 casualties on its first real day in action.

The battalion fought around Messines during the German Spring Offensive of 1918.

It was then moved southwards to support French operations in the Soissons region and its greatest moment came in the capture of Bligny Hill on 6 June 1918, for which feat 1-4/KSLI – reduced to company strength by then – was awarded the French Croix de Guerre avec palme.

In August 1918, it went into the line near Bethune and spent two months there, seeing action on Aubers Ridge before moving to the Somme in October.

November 1918 saw the battalion with 56 Brigade, 19th Division near Bavai, France, when the war ended.

Battle Honours of 1-4th Battalion

France and Flanders 1917; France and Flanders 1918; Passchendaele; Cambrai 1917; Bapaume 1918; Messines 1918; Bailleul; Kemmel; Bligny; Aisne 1918; Cambrai 1918; Selle Valenciennes; Sambre. (14)

The 2-4th Battalion

Formed at Shrewsbury in October 1914, it served on the Isle of Man and then on east coast defences, 1915-17. It was renamed the 50th Provisional Battalion in December 1916. Personnel were absorbed by other battalions by December 1917. No overseas war service.

The 3-4th Battalion

Raised in May 1915 in Shrewsbury, it was stationed in various towns in South Wales, 1915-18.

Restyled the 4th (Reserve) Battalion in April 1916, it was absorbed into the 2nd Herefordshire Regiment in Swansea in 1917 and disbanded at Pembroke Dock at the end of the war. No overseas war service.

The 5th (Service) Battalion

A war-raised service battalion, formed in Shrewsbury in August 1914 under Lieutenant Colonel H. M. Smith, It was drawn from the mass of Kitchener's enthusiastic volunteers coming forward to enlist. Posted to 42 Brigade, 14th Division.

Service Engagements of 5th Battalion on the Western Front to 1918

After further training at Aldershot, it landed at Boulogne on 20 May 1915.

After its first engagement at Ypres on 31 May 1915 it then served entirely on the Western Front.

The 5th Battalion (5/KSLI) saw some of the worst fighting of the war in the Ypres Salient in 1915, around Bellewaerde and Hooge. It was on the Somme in 1916 and saw particularly heavy fighting at Delville Wood and Flers-Courcelette.

After this service it fought at Arras and in the attack on Vimy Ridge in 1917 then returned in August to the Ypres Salient to take part in the Third Battle of Ypres. It was disbanded at Jussy on 4 February 1918, its personnel going to other KSLI battalions.

Battle Honours of 5th Battalion
France and Flanders 1915; France and Flanders 1916; France and Flanders 1917; Ypres 1915; Somme 1916: DelviIIe Wood; Flers-Courcelette; Arras 1917; Ypres 1917. (nine)

The 6th (Service) Battalion
A war-raised service battalion, formed in Shrewsbury in September 1914, posted to 60 Brigade, 20th Division. It landed at Boulogne on 22 July 1915 and then served entirely on the Western Front.

Service Engagements of 6th Battalion on the Western Front to 1918
It fought at Loos in September 1915, around Ypres in 1916 (where it relieved 1/KSLI) and then at the Somme, which included the capture of Guillemont.

It fought at Langemarck (Third Battle of Ypres) in August 1917 and on the Menin Road, Ypres, in September. Served against the Hindenburg Line near Cambrai at the end of the year and throughout the German Spring Offensive in 1918, seeing severe fighting at St Quentin.

The 6th Battalion ended the war north west of Maubeuge, France and was disbanded in Shrewsbury in June 1919.

All remaining 6/KSLI personnel were merged with the 4/KSLI and the Territorial and Shropshire Yeomanry prior to disbandment.

Battle Honours of 6th Battalion
France and Flanders 1915; France and Flanders 1916; France and Flanders 1917; France and Flanders 1918; Mount Sorrel; GuiIIemont; Flers-Courcelette; Le Transloy; Langemarck 1917; Menin Road; Cambrai 1917; St.Quentin; Rosieres. (13)

The 7th (Service) Battalion
A war-raised service battalion under Lieutenant Colonel J.H.Barber, it was formed in Shrewsbury in September 1914 and joined 76 Brigade, 25th Division. It landed at Boulogne on 28 September 1915 and served entirely on the Western Front.

The 7/KSLI first saw action in the Ypres Salient in the winter of 1915-16 and moved to the Somme in July 1916; fighting at Bazentin Ridge and then at Serre on the Ancre later in the year. It was in action at Arras and in the three severe battles of the Scarpe in April and May 1917. Back in the Ypres sector in 1917, 7th Battalion (7/KSLI) took part in the fighting at Polygon Wood in September (Third Battle of Ypres) and was back on the Somme for the battles of 1918. After taking part in the offensives of summer and autumn of 1918, at Albert, Bapaume, the Canal du Nord and the Selle, 7/KSLI ended the war as part of 8 Brigade, 3rd Division, at Romeries, near Solesmes, France. It was disbanded in Shrewsbury in June 1919.

The 7/KSLI suffered more casualties than any other KSLI battalion, with 1048 killed in action or dying during the war. It earned more battle honours than any other KSLI battalion.

Battle Honours of 7th Battalion

France and Flanders 1915; France and Flanders 1916; France and Flanders 1917; France and Flanders 1918; Mount Sorrel; Somme 1916; Albert 1916; Bazentin; Delville Wood; Arras 1917; Scarpe 1917; Arleux; Ypres 1917; Polygon Wood; Somme 1918; St.Quentin; Bapaume 1918; Arras 1918; Lys; Estaires; Hazebrouk; Bethune; Albert 1918; Bapaume 1918; Canal du Nord; Selle. (26)

The 8th (Service) Battalion

A war-raised service battalion, formed in Shrewsbury in September 1914 under Lieutenant Colonel C.H. Sisted. It joined 66 Brigade, 22nd Division and landed in France on 28 October 1915, heading for Amiens. After only a few weeks on the Western Front, 8/KSLI was sent to Macedonia, arriving on 6 November 1915. It spent the remainder of the war on the Salonika front around Doiran, suffering severely from malaria and from its encounters with the enemy. Periods of routine trench work, in reserve along the Struma or in the defences of Salonika were interspersed with some severe fighting such as at Pip Ridge near Lake Doiran, in February 1917 and again in September 1918. The 8th Battalion took part in the final drives against the Bulgarian army in 1918 and after the armistice was sent to Doiran and Dedeagatch and then into Bulgaria. The 8/KSLI ended the war near Stavros and was amalgamated with 2/KSLI on 1 December 1918.

Battle Honours of 8th Battalion

Macedonia 1915-18; Doiran 1917; Doiran 1918 (three)

The 9th Battalion

A reserve battalion, formed at Pembroke Dock in October 1914, it served only in Britain, largely in a training role at Prees Heath camp near Shrewsbury from August 1915.

It had no overseas war service and like the 3rd Battalion, sent trained men to other KSLI battalions and to other units.

The 10th (Shropshire & Cheshire Yeomanry)

Battalion Formed at Cairo on 2 March 1917 from the dismounted troopers of the Shropshire Yeomanry and the Cheshire Yeomanry. Served in Palestine in 231 Brigade, 74th Broken Spur Division. It took part in the second and third battles of Gaza, (July-November 1917), then in operations for the capture of Jerusalem (December 1917) and in the capture of Jericho (February 1918). In the attack on Birj-el-Lisaneh, near Tel Asur, on 10 March 1918, Private Harold Whitfield won the only VC awarded to a Shropshire regiment for the Great War. In May 1918, it went to France, serving on the Lys in August then at Epehy and captured the notorious Quadrilateral in November. Having captured Tournai – where the 53rd Light Infantry had been in action in 1794 – it ended the war near Ath in Belgium and was disbanded in Shrewsbury in June 1919.

Battle Honours of 10th Battalion

France and Flanders 1918; Palestine 1917-18; Epehy; Pursuit to Mons; Gaza; Jerusalem; Jericho; Tel Asur. (eight)

Battle Awards and Medal Honours of 10th Battalion

Private Harold Whitfield, 10th (Shropshire & Cheshire Yeomanry) Battalion.

Award: Victoria Cross Action: Burj-el-Lisaneh, Palestine.

Date: 10 March 1918. London Gazette: 8 May 1918.

Conferred: by HM King George V in Leeds in a public investiture in May 1918.

Private Harold Whitfield, 10th (Shropshire & Cheshire Yeomanry) Battalion.

Fodder for the Guns (Part 2):
British Army Officer Training up to 1914

Such was the nature of warfare in the nineteenth and early twentieth century and given its long history, the British Regular Army employed the format of cavalry charges. This was followed by massed ranks of infantry volley fire. Consequently battles were only ever fought in skirmishes lasting a relatively short duration.

However the bloody, prolonged and mechanised slaughter of the First World War found not only Kitchener's Volunteer Army wanting but also the men leading them.

None of the BEF's commanding officers were adequately experienced or trained in strategic planning in order to fight a sustained 'total' war along a lengthy frontline involving huge numbers of fighting men.

Commanders in Chief, Sir John French and Earl Douglas Haig were both career officers and came from cavalry-trained backgrounds yet had only ever served in small colonial wars.

These small colonial skirmishes, dubbed misleadingly as wars would pale into insignificance when they realized the comprehensive nature of warfare that faced them on the Western Front and elsewhere during the Great War.

Despite not having participated in a mass continental war for over 100 years, the British Army was considered one of the most successful land forces in Europe prior to the Great War, having fought and won every campaign it was involved in. It was not accustomed to failure or defeat at the hands of the enemy.

The Army had grown in response to Kitchener's appeal at such an exponential rate that I.4 million volunteers had swelled its ranks up to 1916. Added to the 500,000 regulars plus reservists this brought the BEF's total strength to over two million men, the great majority of whom were inexperienced amateur soldiers. There was constant mustering and deployment of reinforcements as the scale of casualties depleted whole sections of the frontline. This was to undermine the overall strength of the Allied Force at times when it was crucial to maintain and consolidate hard-won objectives.

Invariably this resulted in bloodbaths and constant changes on the frontline as the better trained and equipped Regular German Army simply brought up reinforcements and recaptured all the ground taken. Sandhurst officers trained for 18 months and Woolwich trained the engineer and gunnery officers over a two-year course. Cadets were required to pay for their education at a cost of £100 per annum and pay for their uniforms and other equipment. No leadership training was given as most came from private schools where they had been taught to lead and serve the country and empire. It was presumed that their respective schools would cover all aspects of team leadership through sports pursuits and layers of prefect hierarchy that was endemic to public school life.

During the conflict the course time was cut to three months in the case of Sandhurst and four in the case of Woolwich as the demand for officers far outstripped supply. As army numbers grew there were 16,000 vacancies at the beginning of the war. The British Staff College, at Camberley in Surrey, that had been dedicated to turning out staff trained officers was shut down in 1914. Since opening in 1858 it had been producing a steady crop of 60 graduates a week. This was woefully inadequate to fill the gap in the ever-expanding BEF in the Great War. Half of its graduates were lost in the trenches in the first few months of fighting. Wellington College, in common with other public schools and educational institutions across the land, formed an Officer Training Corps (OTC) in November 1909 and the driving force locally was the celebrated educationalist Sir John Bayley. Although fully trained in procedure, most OTCs comprised young men of 18 and upwards who were naive about life in general, let alone about leading men into battle, and would go on to suffer devastating casualties. In addition to Wellington College, OTC output was drawn upon heavily across the land as mounting shortages occurred due to casualties at the front.

There could be no adequate training to cover the scale of the trench-based warfare to come in the Great War. The prevalence of lacklustre generalship in the war was put down to a shortage of good staff officers, with many performing the role with no training whatsoever. This was later corrected when staff schools were opened in France and at Cambridge. The successes of 1918 can be attributed to a properly organized staff system handling the logistics of the Army's manifold equipment and supply needs.

No British or European army had ever fought such a war on so many different strategic levels, in such numbers and for such a sustained length of time.

Campaigns, such as the Somme, lasted not for days or weeks but months on end.

It was also customary for high-ranking British officers to visit their own men in the frontline on a regular basis. From 1915 onward, commissioned officers, particularly lieutenants, were expected to lead their men 'over the top' as it was termed in trench warfare and therefore suffered the full might of the enemy gunfire. This invariably happened as they attempted to attack enemy positions across the open space between opposing trenches.

This practice fuelled the casualty rate as German trench snipers lay in wait for just such an event. Their gold braid and red-trimmed uniforms stood out and gave away their rank. These spaces, referred to as no man's land, would sometimes be as little as fifty yards but were mostly hundreds of yards wide. They were also booby trapped with exploding devices including mines, and littered with barbed wire and deadly obstacles designed to hamper an infantry's progress long enough for machine gun positions to draw bead and decimate the enemy's forces. These were very often referred to as killing zones as the majority of infantry losses occurred here. The ritual of leading men over the top was latterly frowned on as clearly the purpose of senior officers was to direct their forces and plan strategic action from a remote and safe distance located many miles behind their own lines.

The creed of hands-on officer participation in warfare was an ingrained tradition in the British Army. It came in with the Duke of Marlborough and should have gone out with the Duke of Wellington at Waterloo. Apparently a senior officer was sitting astride his horse alongside the duke in battle and promptly had his leg blown off by enemy cannonfire, which perhaps underscores the point. Consequently the number of officers, particularly those from the BEF, who became casualties of battle on the Western Front was very high. It resulted in 172 fatalities among the BEF and colonial officers. A total of 78 British and Empire officers, ranked brigadiers general and above died on active service. A further 146 were wounded, making them the highest casualty rates amongst senior officers in proportion to their junior ranks.

The casualty statistics of British officers between 1914 and 1918 are truly appalling. Out of the 247,061 who held the King's commission during the Great War, thirty per cent were wounded, four per cent captured and 13.5 per cent killed. When converted, these figures amount to 116,781, representing nearly fifty per cent of the total strength.

A Brief History of Horses used in the Great War

The British Army's use of horses in the Great War is not, in the main, a tale of a courageous or even noble partnership between man and animal. The original intention was to train horses to make mass cavalry charges but in the event they were used chiefly as beasts of burden hauling field artillery and supplies across war zones purely due to the advent of technology-based strategies.

The first and last major deployment on the Western Front was a single mass engagement resulting in wholesale slaughter of beast and rider in August 1914 at Casteau during the Battle of Mons by the 4th Dragoon Guards of II Corps BEF.

Although initially successful in taking the fight to the enemy, resulting in the first enemy casualty of the war inflicted by lance and sabre, the cavalry were soon overwhelmed and disabled by superior numbers and the use of machine gun batteries.

This was one of the nails in the coffin of the cavalry regiments, which had been pivotal weapons in most of the continental armies' battle tactics for 1,000 years.

Technology and the devastating firepower of modern weapons used in the Great War made their faithful service redundant. Man and horse fell under withering machine gun fire and the resulting carnage demonstrated the dawn of a new age in tactical warfare, which spelt the doom of the cavalry regiments that converted virtually overnight into transport and tank corps battalions.

The role of the horse was however vital as an all-terrain haulage system as they could go where there were no roads and operate in all weathers unlike most mechanical forms of transport. The demands of war also outstripped the supply of mechanised transport leaving the horse as the BEF's only practical alternative heavy haulage across varying battle terrain. Horses would be used in the role of flexible troop support in the Second World War although not in such vast numbers as they were in the Great War and not by the Second World War's reincarnated BEF.

Inevitably they were exposed to just as many dangers as the average infantryman in the frontline of military operations and paid the ultimate price for their blind obedience.

Their sacrifice was great indeed and their demise invariably far removed from the dignity shown to their masters in death. Horses received none of the attendant pomp and reverence afforded to humans when they were interred.

Their rotting carcasses were often left on the roads and byways where they fell, with no more consideration or afterthought shown to them than a worn out pair of boots.

Horsemeat also crept surreptitiously on to soldiers' menus when the usual frontline supplies dried up.

No combatant armies' hands were clean on either side of the divide of war.

This is not to say that the bond between horse and rider wasn't just as strong in the Great War as any other conflict but the first last and only consideration in this new type of warfare was the fighting man, and certainly not his equipment which included the horse. Issues such as equine mortality were treated with lesser importance when men were dying in their tens of thousands. The Army requisitioned all the available horses from local businesses and had the right to take second horses unless proprietors could justify retention on the basis of necessity. In total 1.25 million horses were used by the British in the war with 484,000 killed and injured and almost 750, 000 surviving the carnage.

The majority of surviving horses were sold to Belgian or French farmers to recultivate their damaged lands for crops. Most agricultural economies were near collapse and mass starvation loomed across post-war continental Europe.

The maximum number of horses that could return home with the Army was 60,000.

This meant that out of the one million requisitioned, 75,000 entered the food chain having been sent to the makeshift abattoirs. They used a production line system during which each horse witnessed the demise of the preceding animal in inhumane and often unhygienic circumstances.

In mitigation of the Army's handling of injured horses, when possible equine casualties received first class treatment from the facilities widely available along the frontline.

Twenty hospitals run by the Royal Army Veterinary Corps (RAVC) were set up across the Western Front and the treatment given was first class. The care given by the RAVC extends to all animals connected with the armed services up until today. At a time when no antibiotics existed, the efficacy of simple disinfectants proved remarkably effective.

Of those animal casualties treated, survival rates were in excess of eighty per cent. Yet the inevitable questions remain that cut to the core of human morality. Did we have the right to involve these noble beasts in a war without their consent? Their willing compliance is testament to the devotion they felt towards their human handlers. It is not due to their commitment to the Army or their patriotism or their desire to support the Allied cause and free it from the (human version) of the yoke of tyranny.

The Sourcing of Horses (Regionally and Locally) for the War Effort

For two years prior to the outbreak of the Great war, all the police forces in the UK kept a national census listing the whereabouts of the horse population in anticipation of hostilities that would require them to be commandeered.

At the outbreak, this information was simply handed over to the Army.

Overall the Army estimated it needed up to one million horses to take to France in 1914 and as it only had approximately 25,000 under harness, it rounded up the rest using the police list. During the first year it amassed over 500,000 horses that were sent to army remounting centres at Shirehampton and Liverpool to be retrained army-style for cavalry duties. This was a short and brutal experience that involved first breaking the horse to accept a rider, then teaching them cavalry and army-style draft pulling methods. The greatest need was for light draft horses to pull artillery pieces across land, so the biggest requisitioner was the Royal Horse Artillery.

Since they were already on the police list, horses local to Wellington were simply commandeered from small businesses as well as being sourced from Shrewsbury through the town's massive livestock market.

At first the local supply held up with some complaints from businesses that used four horses but were often left with just one to complete their orders. This affected farmers, draymen and freight haulers across the town and region. However, demand was far outstripping supply and the local livestock market in Wellington run by Barber & Son of Church Street could not source sufficient numbers from the breeding stock and dealers.

Barber & Sons at the weekly livestock market in Wellington

As the war progressed the tally of horses required by the army rose to more than two million and businesses that relied on horsepower were revisited and stripped of more of their animals.

Many firms, especially those that delivered goods or materials were affected badly. The reduction in trade caused severe hardship and in some cases, closure.

Shukers, a local car supplier, was quick to take advantage and started suggesting automotive power as the logical successor to horsepower.

Although fuel shortages did restrict the scope and introduction of automotives, this would herald the decline of horsepower and the rise of heavy haulage vehicles evident post 1918.

The Journal: *Shuker car advert*

War News as Reported in *The Journal*

These extracts from *The Journal* in August and October 1914 reveal the kindness shown both nationally and locally by Britain to the plight of the Belgians who were among the first to endure mass suffering during the war.

Belgian Refugees Arrive in Wellington

The first five families of Belgian refugees arrive in Wellington and were accommodated in private homes in Park Street and Watling Street. Among their number is the Francis family of Wespelain, four of whose children went missing when the Germans arrived at their small holding. They lost everything when their home and cattle were confiscated but managed to escape with their two boys, aged six and four.

Above: **The Journal** *(24/10/14)* – **Belgian refugees, the Francis family of Wespelain**

Left: **Belgian family in Wellington** – **The Journal** *(24/10/14)*

This Belgian family, at present occupying a house in Watling Street, Wellington had a terrible experience when fleeing from the Germans in the Louvain District. The flight lasted for five days, their only shelter being such as the hedgerows provided. Only on one occasion did they sleep beneath a roof, and that a church. During this fearful ordeal their only nourishment consisted of scraps of food picked up from the roads over which the troops had previously passed.

Early Victories and Downplayed Defeats

With the battlelines drawn firmly behind trenches, the Western Front campaign was in danger of drifting into stalemate; destined to become a lengthy war of attrition.

To keep up morale at home the newspapers were encouraged to seize on any item of news that put the Allies, or more specifically the BEF, in a positive light.

This was evidenced in the following news item dated 30 January 1915:   Allied attack at La Bassee as reported in *The Journal* (Headline) *Sunday* Title*: British Success at La Bassee Another attack was today made on the British position near La Bassee and met with the same fate as that reported last Thursday, except that the enemy this time were beaten off more easily. All the lost trenches were reoccupied; Cuinchy, a couple of miles to the south-west of La Bassee was the scene of the encounter and while the Germans, attacking with three battalions, left two hundred dead in front of our trenches, the British loss was small. A more favourable result for them attended a German offensive in the Argonne, where the French fell back for 800 yards and organised a fresh line of defence. A French official message summarising events down to 26th January said the allies were constantly reinforcing their armies; their offensive power was daily increasing and they would make their maximum effort when they had the maximum of means.*

Such reports were carefully constructed to leave *Journal* readers glowing with admiration for our bold Allied efforts at the front. However, if they analysed the information more closely they would realize that it told them very little about the overall progress of the war or even when any major objective was likely to be achieved. Government control of the press under the statutory provisions of DORA was such that all war-related news was censored if considered too sensitive or overtly detailed with specific facts that may lead to the undermining of public morale or the disclosure of vital information to enemy agents supposedly operating in the UK.

Gallipoli: A Land Bridge Too Far
(A Tragedy of Allied Self Deception)

The entrance to the Dardanelles lies at the north eastern corner of the Aegean sea above the Mediterranean between Italy and Greece, forming part of Turkey's coastline. The Dardanelles comprise a narrow strait, which on the western side leads to a broad eponymous headland of the town, Gallipoli. Once past this commanding feature the strait broadens out into the Sea of Marmara. The ancient city of Istanbul also

Diagrammatic map of the Dardanelles region - 1915

known as Constantinople, depending on whether it had been captured by Christian or Muslim forces, lies at its northern head straddling the Bosphorus Strait. This in turn, forms another strait (Bogaz Hatti) stretching directly northwards forcing its way between a narrow land bridge between the old world and the new: Europe via Bulgaria and the Middle East via Turkey.

In 1915 the capture of the Gallipoli peninsula and the great prize of Istanbul beyond it, were regarded by the Allies as vital strategically. It was viewed as a possible back door supply route to Russia, which was busily fighting the German/Austro-Hungarian forces on the Eastern Front. If the Allies held the Dardanelles they not only controlled the sea traffic in or out but they could also hold the military upper hand across the whole region.

Even as the serving war poet Rupert Brooke lay dying of septicemia on his troopship bound for Gallipoli, the first seeds of doubt were sown about the success of this Allied operation, which was spearheaded by the British, French and Anzac (Australian and New Zealand) forces. Indeed the loss of a British cruiser and a French submarine to a minefield laid in the Dardanelles prior to the commencement of the operation should have set alarm bells ringing.

The British realized too late that the nearest deepwater supply and repair harbour was Alexandria in Egypt, over seven hundred miles south from the entrance to the Dardanelles. However, as these narrow straits form part of the border between Europe and Turkey they were inevitably going to attract attention as a possible site for a campaign of Allied action at some point during the war. Britain's military was heavily involved in the region and the Royal Navy had several bases dotted about the Mediterranean including Gibraltar, Malta, Cyprus, Alexandria and Suez. Policing those interests required unhindered passage across all parts of this busy sea and the German alliance with Ottoman Turkey threatened to disrupt this vital traffic.

Destroying their supply route via the Berlin to Baghdad railway was seen as an essential next step and key to the successful invasion of Mesopotamia so as to secure Allied interests in its vast oil fields. As First Lord of the Admiralty in Asquith's wartime coalition cabinet, Winston Churchill suggested this action as a means of slicing this central alliance in two and also providing the Allies with a practical means to assist Russia's war effort.

In league with other MPs Churchill also made the case that as Austro-Hungarian troops had attacked Russia's eastern flank in the Caucasus in late 1914 and then had formally asked for assistance, they were honour bound to respond to this plea.

This operation came at a critical time for the Allies as a means of breaking the current mood of pessimism caused by the trenchbound stalemate on the Western Front. Scoring a much-needed victory was seen as a way of demoralising the enemy and a practical way of dislocating Germany's links with the Middle East via the Ottoman Empire, thus weakening its sphere of influence in this part of the

Winston Churchill - First Lord of the Admiralty 1915

world. It was also predicated on the false assumptions that Germany's forces needed bolstering to continue fighting the war and that a new supply route to Russia was logistically possible.

A seemingly simple operation on paper was undermined by several weaknesses in the Allied plan not least being the total lack of funding and strategic planning.

Firstly and decisively the task force was vastly underequipped with manpower, weaponry and ammunition. There was no real hope of relief or supplies in sufficient quantity to secure and hold any bridgehead made. Secondly there was a woeful lack of local intelligence as to the disposition and strength of the forces ranged against them. Their opponents were well led and comprised a crack division of German soldiers and Turkish fanatics fighting to protect their home territory. There was no coherent Allied plan of attack and no clear list of strategic objectives. Although able and experienced, the officer in charge, Major General Sir Ian Hamilton, decided to blame everyone else when things inevitably went catastrophically awry.

The first Anglo-French landings were made at Cape Helles in April 1915 and the forces initially started to make headway inland.

Major General Sir Ian Hamilton,
CIC of Gallipoli campaign –
circa 1915

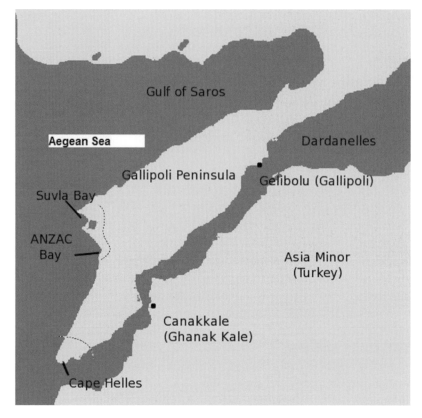

Allied landings at Suvla Bay - Gallipoli 1915

However they met increasingly heavy opposition and had to retreat back to the beaches.

The sheer cliffs surrounding the one shallow cove on the peninsula at Suvla Bay meant that the opposing force, under German direction and led by the brilliant Turkish general Mustafa Kemal (later to become Ataturk - the father of modern Turkey) could simply pound the invaders as they tried to storm the beach.

The Australians took the Aegean route and came ashore at what they later renamed Anzac Bay and encountered similar heavy resistance. The initial casualty rate ran to seventy per cent with the sea turning red with blood until a bridgehead could be established. It was to be several weeks before any reinforcements arrived by which time every Allied

Mustapha Kemal (Ataturk)

attack had been countered successfully, thus producing a stalemate position lasting for several fruitless months.

Hamilton's successor Sir Charles Munro recommended withdrawal immediately, which was reluctantly agreed to by the war cabinet in early December.

After nine months of attritional deadlock and slaughter, the Allies evacuated under cover of darkness on successive nights in December 1915 and early January 1916, surprisingly without a single loss of life. The campaign's disastrous failure resulted in 250,000 casualties comprising 27,000 French and 35,000 Anzacs dead. It is rightly claimed by the Anzacs as a national tragedy with its own day of commemoration.

Once the scale of the overall allied losses became evident, Churchill was so appalled at his own folly he resigned his post to fight in the trenches of the Western Front.

Overall it was a foolhardy and naively conceived operation as the net result was that, far from being knocked out of the war, Turkey went on to fight almost to the very end. The impracticality of this strategy demonstrated that this mythical back door supply route to Russia was entirely erroneous and therefore undeliverable.

Churchill's resignation from the government was a curious move politically speaking, yet the integrity of his actions fostered great popularity for him nationally, particularly with the common soldier and the man in the street. It could therefore be viewed as a shrewd manoeuvre on his part. He departed for the Western Front yet retained his position as an MP, which could afford him a vital route back to the centre of power politics in Westminster. In a characteristically brave move (perhaps tinged with a deathwish) he was attached to the Grenadier Guards and on 5 January 1916 he took command of the 6th Battalion, Royal Scots Fusiliers.

He was an experienced soldier and at great personal risk achieved success in the trenches at the head of his battalion. The irony was that in his sector near Ypres at Ploegsteert lay the German-held town of Messines, where a certain corporal named Adolf Hitler was also manning his own trench. Having assuaged a guilty conscience and won his battle spurs, Churchill was tiring of the rigours of combat command. He began to hunger for the corridors of power and looked for a way back into Westminster politics. David Lloyd George was to tempt him back in 1917 and as Prime Minister, offer him the post of Minister for Munitions, which ironically was the post Lloyd George had held under Asquith.

Winston Churchill (centre) - commander 6/Royals - 1916

Churchill agreed readily and made a spectacular success of the job thus cementing the rebuilding of his own political credentials and restoring his public reputation.

The War at Sea (Extract 1):
News Reports Naval Engagements as Reported in
The Wellington Journal

Up until the end of 1914 and into 1915 the physical reporting of the war at sea had been minimal as the greatly anticipated trial of strength between the British Navy's Grand Fleet, ranked as the envy of the world and the German High Seas Fleet, had so far not materialised. After all wasn't the massive strike, the 'bloody nose' that Asquith boasted would bring the upstart kaiser to his knees long overdue? The nation needed retribution to be wrought in revenge for the bombardments carried out by the German Navy on some of the north east's coastal towns early on in the war, which were vicious, unprovoked and caused great damage and some fatalities. The attack took place in December 1914 on the coastal towns of Whitby, Scarborough and Hartlepool resulting in 119 civilian deaths.

The Journal along with other regional newspapers were spoonfed selected stories by the War Office and were just as heavily censored to reflect a positive spin to events, as well as adding a local flavour, as the following examples show.

The Journal report of 26 September 1914 reported:

Wellingtonian With the Fleet

The majority of Wellingtonians who are serving their King and country are doing so in the land forces but the town has also contributed a few to the Navy. One is now serving on a battleship in the North Sea, and in one of his letters received by a brother this week the writer points out how anxious officers and men are for a really tiptop naval engagement with the Germans. The writer says: 'All our boys are longing for 'the day' as Kaiser Bill puts it. We are doing a great deal of work, and are anxiously watching and waiting. Our squadron took part in the scrap off Heligoland.* That was alright but we want the real thing. We are all as fit as it is possible to be and are longing for a smack at the Germans. The land forces are doing well and we are waiting for an opportunity to play our part. We are not allowed to say much in our letters home, but when the Kaiser's Fleet tackles our front line there will be some startling news for you.

*This Wellingtonian letter-writer serving in the Navy and referring to a 'scrap' his ship was involved with off Heligoland [Danish islands in the North Sea] was a natural follow-on to a war news report in the previous week's *Journal* war describing the action as follows:

One of the most brilliant feats of the war up to the present was the daring raid by a force of British Destroyers and Cruisers on Friday last week, during a thick mist, upon a greatly superior number of German gunboats in the dangerous mined waters off Heligoland, whereby but with slight injury to our ships, a signal defeat was inflicted on the enemy, four of whose vessels were sunk and others put out of action.

The pitch of reader excitement was ratcheted up with reports of ever

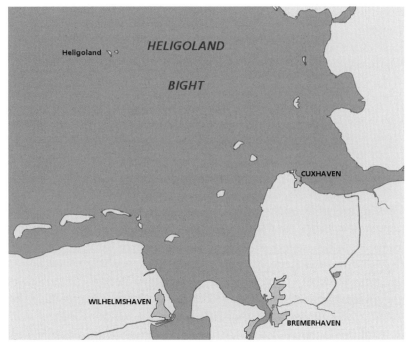

Map showing location of Heligoland (Danish Islands)

more dramatic naval engagements such as the following edited
compilation of reports published in *The Journal* on 30 January 1915:

British Naval Success in the North Sea

*The admiralty has made the following announcement – early this
morning a British patrolling squadron of battle cruisers and light
cruisers, under vice-admiral Sir David Beatty with a destroyer flotilla
under Commodore Tyrwhitt, sighted four German battle cruisers
several light cruisers and a number of destroyers steering South-
westerly about 14 miles from their position and apparently making for
the British coast. Action engaged about 9:30am between the cruisers,
Lion, Tiger, Princess Royal, New Zealand and Indomitable against
cruisers, Derslinger, Seydlitz, Moltke and Bluecher. During a well-
contested running fight – about 1pm the Battle Cruiser Bluecher, which
had fallen out of line, was seen to capsize and sink. Admiral Beatty
also reported that two other German battle cruisers were seriously*

damaged. No British ships were lost. Lion led the attack suffering 11 wounded and none dead. The only other British naval officer killed in this action was Commander Taylor of HMS Tiger. He was the youngest son of the Rev. A.L. Taylor, for many years Headmaster of Ruabon Grammar School and prior to the outbreak of the war was in charge of the Royal Naval College, Keyham, Devonport. He was a good all-round athlete in his younger days and played for Wales in international rugby matches. One hundred and twenty-three survivors were rescued from the 885 crew members of the Bluecher and it is possible that others have been saved by some of our Destroyers. No other reports of Destroyer or light-cruiser fighting have been received at the admiralty, though some has taken place. Their Lordships have expressed their satisfaction to Vice-Admiral Sir David Beatty.

War Reports from Wellingtonians: Letters, Diaries and Personal Accounts: Letter home from Private W.J. Smith as published in *The Journal*, 17 October 1914

Private W.J Smith (aged 22) of the Royal Marines, writing to his mother at Charlton:

We came from the firing line straight to England to reorganized the battalions. There are only 150 of our battalion left; Only 9 in our platoon out of 31, and only myself out of our section. We had to retire from Antwerp and when we had got away, as we thought, they threw our train off the rails and then attacked us but we got away. We walked 50 miles in 30 hours: indeed in total we marched 61 miles. We were walking two nights and two days. We had 100 shells in two hours over our trenches and they don't half make a noise; they whistle past your head; you can't guess what it is like! The only thing I am glad about is that I am alive, as I had some near shaves.

Private W.J. Smith

He enclosed with his note a piece of a German Zeppelin which he asked his mother to keep as a memento.

Personal Accounts of Wellington's Fighting Men

Another Wellingtonian – David Barnett – has studied the social and wartime history of his own family, in particular his great uncles and their friends who all enlisted in the First World War. Their stories as told to me by David, were partly sourced from his cousin, Verna Ray and his Great Aunt Alice Taylor (née Barnett), who kept a notebook throughout the period. Their stories are remarkable in that all five survived the war to return home.

Five Wellington lads went off to the Great War: two sets of brothers and a friend, all pals and local to the Newdale area. They were hoping to serve together in a short fight and return home as heroes. The heroic part came true but despite this valiant service they never got to serve alongside one another. The five were: Frederick 'Fred' William Barnett, his brother Joseph Stanley 'Stan' Barnett; James Leonard 'Len' Rigby, his younger brother William H. 'Billy' Rigby and their pal Tom Green. Their stories are told individually.

Fred (back row, third from left) and Friends, 16th Lancers – in training at Aldershot, 1914

Private 51042, Frederick William Barnett (MM) Machine Gun Corps and 16th Lancers

Fred joined up on 3 September 1914 and was seconded to the 16th Lancers He was wounded whilst in the Lancers in 1915 and after convalescing at home he went back to war and transferred into the Machine Gun Corps [MGC] – but soon learned they had a bit of an adverse reputation. Knowing what Uncle Fred was like I bet he thought he would give the enemy a taste of their own medicine.

The Corps was nicknamed the suicide squad. If the Germans captured you, they did not take you prisoner – they shot you. While serving in the MGC Fred won the Military Medal. No one in the family seemed to know about this until my research uncovered the salient facts. The Military Medal award to Fred was announced in

Fred Barnett – MGC – later of 16th Lancers

the *London Gazette* issue 30573, page 3227m dated 12 March 1918. The citation reads: The military decoration was awarded to Private F.W. Barnett – 51042, for acts of gallantry and devotion to duty under fire or for individual or associated acts of bravery which were insufficient to merit the Distinguished Conduct Medal.

F.W. Barnett has further earned the right to add the letters MM to his name. His Majesty the King has been pleased to approve the award of the Military Medal to the mentioned non-commissioned officers and men. (Service: British Army, Regiment: Machine Gun Corps.)

When Fred returned from the war he became a policeman and served on Merseyside.

Private Joseph Stanley Barnett - 4th Battalion KSLI and 7th Leinsters

Stan's war experiences were very different. Having gone with Billy Rigby to Shrewsbury on

J.S. 'Stan' Barnett, 4/KSLI and later 7th Leinsters

J.S. 'Stan' Barnett – KSLI group training at Pembroke Docks, prior to embarkation to France. [Stan is on the front row second from the left]

3 March 1917 to enlist and serve together, only Stan managed to join the KSLI.

He was with his company in Ypres on 31 July 1917 when he was wounded at the railway station. Having suffered a German bombardment his whole regiment was affected.

"They all got blown up," said his daughter Verna Ray. "They threw him on the pile with the dead. He had his gas mask on and by chance they saw blood bubbling through it. He didn't talk much about it, but he told me he got hit in the face and on the wrist. The scars on his cheekbone and wrist faded over the years."

Stan Barnett shrapnel, tag date should read 1917

He kept the piece of shrapnel that was removed from his face and the family retained it.

When he returned after convalescence in Richmond, Surrey he was reassigned to the 7th Leinsters and served in Ireland. After the war he became a farmer in Hadley in Telford'.

James Leonard Rigby - Army Service Corps Len Rigby was a local friend and joined the Army Service Corps on 9 December 1915.

From his signing on record his pay was six shillings [30p] per day. His service details are unknown but we do know he survived the war, married and had children. He was a big man with the old Lilywhites [Wellington Town Football Club]. I knew him well – he was assistant trainer and did all sorts of other things for them.

Private 48179, William.H. Rigby (MM) – 10th Battalion, South Wales Borderers

Billy Rigby was Len's younger brother and joined up with Stan on 3 March 1917, but despite asking to serve together, Billy was put into the 10th Battalion, South Wales Borderers (SWB).

W.H. 'Billy' Rigby, 10th Battalion South Wales Borderers – standing on the left with a pal

W.H. 'Billy' Rigby – seated second from left with three pals

He was awarded the Military Medal and was later twice mentioned in despatches which added oak leaves to his MM decoration. The SWB regimental diary extract for the date 20 October 1918 reads:

'48179 Pte. W. H. Rigby awarded M.M. Details : 18/10/18 – at 05:00 Hours, a fighting patrol of 24 O.Rs (other ranks) under 2nd Lt.Ruthers crossed river Selle near Troisville with objective of holding Quarry K until relieved by a platoon of 14th Battalion Royal Welch Regiment (due at 18:00 Hours). They reached the Quarry and found it occupied by the enemy with a M.G. Crew. After careful reconnaissance they attacked with bombs and succeeded in capturing the Quarry, killing the garrison, after which the objective was consolidated with 4 posts being established around same. After 20 minutes the enemy counter-attacked wounding 2nd Lt. Ruthers and 5 O.Rs. Owing to the danger of being cut off our party withdrew from its position.'

Billy went on to serve in India until 1922 when he returned to England and married and had children. His son Hardy donated his medals to the SWB regimental museum [The Regimental Museum of the Royal Welsh] at their Brecon HQ in 1998 after his death.

Thomas Green - Motor Transport Army Service Corps

Last of the five was Tom Green, although we weren't able to pin down where he lived, only that on 11 December 1915 he joined the Motor Transport Army Service Corps.

He became ill and was invalided out on 11 February 1918 and was awarded the Silver Badge Number 513944 – so idiots wouldn't rush up in the street and give him a white feather [a symbol of cowardice]. Tom visited my Aunt Alice on 23 January while she was working for the Landers family at Oakley, Haygate Road, Wellington.

Five local lads and friends who joined up and who all survived and served their country proudly in The Great War.

A Wellington Serviceman's Letter Home to Family, as reported in *The Journal*

The following letter was published in *The Journal* on 10 October 1914:

Wellingtonian Wounded in the War

Last week it was reported that Second Lieutenant H.L. Paddock (son of Mr & Mrs G.H. Paddock of the Hollies, Wellington) had been wounded while operating with the Sherwood Foresters in the Battle of the Aisne. At that time the precise nature of the injury had not been ascertained, but this is made definite by a letter received on Thursday by Mr & Mrs Paddock* in which their gallant son says: "The doctors have now removed the shrapnel bullet and I am going on well, except that the wound (in a thigh) burns like fire. It does so while I am writing. I wish the Kaiser had the bullet in his head!' With humorous optimism, which appears to have characterised the British 'Tommy' all along, Lieutenant Paddock (for his promotion was gazetted on Wednesday) concludes his letter with the hope that his favourite cat 'Toby' is still innocent of the vicissitudes of warfare and is going on alright. (*The same G.H. Paddock of the Wellington Volunteer Civilian Corps (VCC) [Home Guard].)

He recovered and returned to combat being subsequently promoted to the rank of captain and then to major, for the versatile skills and daring he applied fearlessly to his many wartime exploits. Tragically, this local hero suffered further wounds and was later killed in action.

His sacrifice is recorded on the Wellington Lych Gate Memorial.

The entry in the Wrekin role of honour reads:-

PA/2724 - Major Henry Leslie Paddock - The Sherwood Foresters (Notts and Derbys Regiment) attached to 4th Battalion, The East

Lancs Regiment. Only son of E.A. and G.H. Paddock, The Hollies, Haygate Road, Wellington, killed in action in Flanders 23rd March 1918. He joined the army in 1914 and received a commission as 2nd Lieutenant and saw much action in France. Such was his fearless disposition that he was entrusted with extremely hazardous duties during which he was wounded in the leg and the eye. He gained promotion to Captain and subsequently to Major - died aged 27'.

War News - as Reported in *The Journal*, 1915

Successes in Gallipoli

A French Communiqué dealing with the operations in Gallipoli stated that British Forces had landed successfully near the bay of Suvla and made progress in the region of Gaba Tepe, where after violent fighting, they gained a footing on the slopes of Sari Bair.

More Gains in Gallipoli (Wednesday)

Sir Ian Hamilton reported a gain of 500 yards in the Gallipoli peninsula, in the region of Suvla where fresh troops were landed recently. 'Heavy attacks against the right flank of the 'Anzac' army's positions in the northern zone had been repulsed. The situation in the southern zone remained unchanged.

The following is an extract of War News from *The Journal* dated 15 November 1915:

Churchill Resigns

The Press Bureau has released the following letters which passed between Rt. Hon. Winston Churchill and the Prime Minister (H.H. Asquith):

Nov. 11 - My dear Asquith, When I left the Admiralty five months ago I accepted an office with few duties, at your request, to take part in the work of the war council and to assist new ministers with the knowledge of current operations which I then possessed in a special degree. The counsels which I have offered are upon record in the minutes of the Committee of Imperial Defence and in the memoranda I have circulated to the cabinet, and I draw your attention at the present time to these. I am in cordial agreement with the decision to form a small war council. I appreciated the intention you expressed to me six weeks ago to include me among the members. I foresaw then the personal difficulties which you would have to face in its composition and I make no complaint that your scheme should be changed. But with that change, my work in the government comes naturally to a close. Knowing what I do about the present situation and the instruments of executive power, I could not accept a position of general responsibility for war policy without any effective share of its guidance and control. Even when decisions of principle are rightly taken the speed and method of their execution are factors which determine the result. Nor do I feel able in times like these to remain in well-paid inactivity.

I therefore ask you to submit my resignation to the king. I am an officer and place myself unreservedly at the disposal of the military authorities, observing that my regiment is in France. I have a clear conscience, which enables me to bear responsibilities for past events with composure. Time will vindicate my administration of the admiralty, assign me my due share in the vast preparations and operations which have secured for us the command of the seas. With much respect and unaltered friendship – I bid you goodbye. Yours very sincerely, (signed) Winston S. Churchill.

(Asquith's reply came swiftly) Nov 12:

My dear Churchill, I hoped that you would reconsider your decision and regret to learn from your letter that you have not felt able to do so. You have rendered services both in council and in administration which no-one is better able to appreciate than myself in regard to the conduct and direction of the war and I am sincerely grieved that you should think it your duty to leave the cabinet. I am certain that you will continue to take an active and effective part in the prosecution of the war. As you know well, on personal grounds, I feel acutely the severance of our long association.

Yours always sincerely

(signed) H.H. Asquith

CHAPTER 4 - 1916

Waste

'The fight must be to the finish - to a knockout.'

(David Lloyd George.
Prime Minister in interview with journalist Roy W.
Howard in September 1916.)

The War At Sea: (Extract 2): The Battle of Jutland – The German Fleet's Wasted Opportunity

The war at sea was to culminate in the only major naval engagement on the high seas between the main antagonists Germany and Britain whose massive fleets met off Jutland (known to the Germans as Skagerrak), Denmark on 31 May 1916.

The newly appointed Royal Navy commander, Admiral Sir John Jellicoe, knew he had to be cautious as Churchill had warned him he 'could lose the war in an afternoon'.

In the end it was not a decisive encounter as the

Map of Jutland sea battle, 1916

British suffered heavy casualties in manpower and warships. Nevertheless, Jellicoe's Grand Fleet chased down the German High Seas Fleet under *Vizeadmiral* Reinhard Scheer and forced a retreat, thereby winning the day as well as the psychological war of nerves thus far. Both sides claimed victory but it was Jellicoe's Grand Fleet that was to maintain mastery of the sea routes and the approaches to the coastline, thus fully protecting the British Isles.

Admiral Sir John Jellicoe

On paper the Germans were the victors of the Jutland encounter with 14 British warships sunk for 6,094 killed whilst they in turn lost 10 warships for 2,551 killed. The Kaiser however, was so appalled and disappointed with his fleet's performance that they were ordered back to their home base and were never allowed to make a show of force during the conflict, again relying on their submarine fleet to continue the war at sea.

'Wholesale Slaughter on the Battlefields' (as reported in the local press - including *The Journal*)

Although heavily constrained by the provisions of DORA, the local press seemed to have been given freedom to print explicit reports of battles as well as casualty lists and where possible, accompanying photos of the victims.

Casualty lists of local men were starting to be printed on a regular and alarming basis. There was growing public disquiet about the amount of lives being sacrificed to achieve a successful outcome to the war. Prior to the outbreak, victory had never been in doubt.

Waste of life on the Western Front (including Wellingtonians) Somme Campaign July–Nov 1916: (Part 1)

The word 'battle' is a misnomer as the Somme was not a single engagement but a series of long attritional battles culminating in an Allied success achieved for the princely sum of seven miles of captured territory. Few guessed at the time that it was to become an infamous

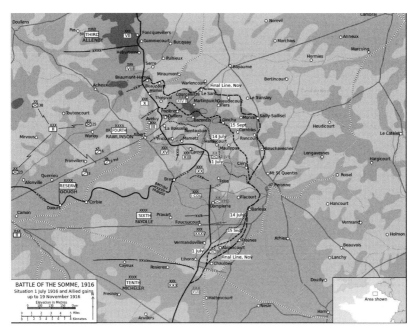

BATTLE OF THE SOMME, 1916
Situation 1 July 1916 and Allied gains
up to 19 November 1916

Somme battleground map, circa 1916

byword for slaughter as one of the bloodiest campaigns of the entire war.

This notorious operation occurred at a crucial time for the BEF and also the French. As part of the German Spring Offensive of 1916, the operation to attack Verdun and its ring of defensive forts was codenamed *Gericht* (judgement) and commenced with a *trommelfeuer* (drum fire) bombardment of one million shells. Their troops took back most of the earlier Allied gains and inflicted a terrible defeat on the French Army, especially during the fall of the strongest fort at Douaumont that resulted in huge numbers of dead and wounded.

Marshal Joffre appointed General Philippe Petain,* a stolid infantryman, to lead the fight-back at Verdun. He became the author of the famous rallying cry *'Ils ne passeront pas'* (they shall not pass). His dogged counter-offensive

*Marshal Joseph Jacques Césaire
Joffre, Knight Grand Cross;
Order of Merit (GCB OM)*

campaign of Verdun, even though successful, was still being fought into November of that same year.

[*This same French hero was to make a devil's bargain with another generation of Germans in the Second World War.]

As the Allied commander, Joffre was desperately looking to build up morale with a fresh campaign on the Western Front to compensate for the devastating losses by the French during the Verdun affair and the area around the Somme looked promising.

The BEF under Sir Douglas Haig were to spearhead an attack along a twenty-mile front either side of the Somme river with multiple objectives that would prove to be the campaign's initial undoing. Haig had also planned a big push through to the Ypres Salient some forty miles from Brussels northwards above the Somme after first 'mopping up' the Germans. He left the main strategic operational planning to his second in command Major General Henry Rawlinson. Whilst

General - later Marshal - Philip Petain aka the Lion of Verdun

Haig commanded great respect from his men throughout the war, one of his biggest faults was his inattention to strategic matters that should have led him to question the finer details of these battle plans more closely.

Rawlinson was inclined to react badly to criticism and tended to devise his own tactics. This resulted inevitably in haphazard results across most of the Western Front campaigns involving the BEF and combined Allied operations up to that point.

The second problem faced by Haig was the state of readiness of his own forces that had to deliver this much needed Allied success on an otherwise deadlocked Western Front. The BEF itself comprised three elements: the regulars; the Kitchener volunteer inductees who vastly outnumbered the regulars; and the

General H. Rawlinson

raw recruits who had been drafted in March 1916 as conscription was introduced for the first time in British civil or military history. This was felt to be a necessary measure designed to bolster numbers from previous losses and increase the overall strength of the BEF to almost two million men.

Even the regular infantry soldiers lacked the necessary fieldcraft skills required for the Western Front as no modern army had fought in such vast battlefield campaigns before. Trench warfare had never been so comprehensive with booby traps, mines and barbed wire as well as dugouts and gun emplacements so well engineered by the Germans. The overall lack of skills was to weigh heavily against the BEF in this first of many combined Allied operations that would later bear the hallmark of success in the closing campaigns of the war.

The Somme offensive began on 1 July. It followed a week-long heavy bombardment of the enemy positions by British artillery designed to destroy the forward trenches and deplete the German gun emplacements as well as open up the ground for the infantry. Between 24 and 30 June, over a million shells were fired in one of the longest bombardments in British artillery history up to that point in time.

An example of a fortified German trench bunkers

However, unbeknownst to Haig or the Allies, up to a third of the shells had failed to explode or else missed their targets.

The British field artillery were just as green as the infantry and did not have a consistent method of range-finding to help guide their fire directly onto enemy positions. The ballistics methodology for the succeeding battles in the Great War was developed by the Royal Artillery and Royal Field Artillery and became standard practice in the Second World War; with spotting by radio added.

The Allies also miscalculated the resilience of German trench emplacements. The *Bosch* engineers were diligent and built them several metres deep complete with fortified blockhouses every 30 to 50 metres, made out of strengthened concrete and bricks.

The bombardment was largely ineffective as the German infantry and gunners, machine and artillery simply hunkered down in their fortified bunkers deep underground and waited for the shelling to stop. Once the all clear sounded they emerged and resumed their positions behind their nests of machine guns. Their next cue was the British officers' whistles as they marshalled their infantry section by section prior to going over the top, giving the perfect prompt to German machine gunners to fire.

The slaughter began at 7:30 am, as the final element of this epic tragedy slotted into place. Believing that the German infantry had been eliminated the BEF's standard practice was to send in infantry in single line formation across no man's land on a broad front in three waves. The Allies, including Haig himself, fatally underestimated the capabilities of the opposition and were soon to discover they were up against a highly mechanised, well-equipped and experienced professional German infantry.

1 July 1916 was the blackest day in the history of the British Army and it still holds the record for the heaviest casualties suffered in a single day's engagement. It soon became clear that the objectives for the first day were too many and too varied to be carried out successfully in order to make enough co-ordinated progress along the wide battlefront. It was vital to consolidate any gains in order to resist the inevitable German counter-offensive.

Barring a few unsupported successes in the south, the BEF failed to achieve their objectives across the battlefront and the Allied offensive ground to a halt.

One of the few achievements on the first day was the capture of Thiepval by 18th Division. This was achieved under the command of the brilliant army trainer Major General Sir Ivor Maxse.

His division was the only one to conduct practice briefings of the attack 24 hours prior

Major General
Sir Ivor Maxse

to the actual operation. The applied method of creeping barrage was also to save lives. This involved a steady barrage of artillery fire aimed just ahead of the troops and moving forward at the same rate, acting as a protective curtain across no man's land and was adopted as standard practice for future BEF engagements.

The open plain to the west of the river was to prove the main killing ground for the Allied casualties. The Germans had established lines of machine gun posts which worked in unison and were angled across no man's land. The terrain sometimes narrowed to only a few hundred yards between trench lines which the Germans exploited to the full.

They produced murderous and concentrated *enfilades* (crossfire), between machine gun positions, aimed at waist height. The British infantry's basic tactic of forward advance by single lines had the simple objective of reaching the enemy's trench and capturing the occupants by sections. The attack, usually in three waves at timed intervals, was to prove predictably fruitful for the German machine gunners.

The impact was demoralising as the slaughter of each wave was witnessed by those following behind. Some realized they were marching to their deaths and dying for nothing. To refuse to go over the top was mutiny, which meant automatic court martial and summary execution for cowardice, so the choice boiled down to death by either British or German bullet. Most opted for the latter and went over the top to do their bit before being scythed down like 'wheat at harvest time', as the German gunners would later describe their slaughter. They did so if only for the sake of the promised war pensions for their families. When faced with certain death the mind focuses quickly on the only positives remaining. This whole campaign was to prove the defining moment in the career of Field Marshal Haig. Due to the sacrifice paid by the infantry he was referred to in some circles as the 'Butcher of the Somme'. The total number of British casualties on that first day, 1 July was 19,741 dead and 40,885 wounded or missing. Yet despite subsequent dubious battle campaigns, which cost further great losses of manpower for little material gain, Haig was to maintain his popularity among his general staff and other ranks for the duration of the war. His own relentless 'single decisive blow' notions persisted even after the Somme campaign and were based on the false contention that the German military machine was close to collapse and only required a single decisive hammer blow to be delivered by the BEF as the main force. This was fuelled by misleading information supplied by his head of Intelligence, John Charteris. Haig aniticapted that this would destroy the Germans will to fight and they would quickly call an armistice to sue for peace.

Haig had always planned to send in the reserve cavalry regiment on the first day of the Somme but given the disastrous outcome they were rendered permanently redundant.

The rest of the campaign was therefore doomed to become a series of attritional battles with attacks and counter attacks moving the line back and forth and resulting in stalemate.

The poor progress and the growing casualty lists fomented distrust at home from the war cabinet and the new Prime Minister, Lloyd George.

The lush farmland of the Thiepval estate and village, a once rich manor at the heart of the Somme killing fields, was totally destroyed. Nine other villages dotted across the region were wiped off the map

The Thiepval Memorial, near the Somme, Northern France

by the ebb and flow of battle, not just as a result of this first Somme campaign but of the hostilities as a whole.

After the war one of the largest First World War memorials was built near Thiepval and designed by the renowned architect Sir Edwin Lutyens. It was dedicated to the 72,000 Allied soldiers from this costly campaign who were missing, presumed dead.The name of Wellington serviceman Private Samuel Harris (of whom we will hear more later) also appears on this memorial.

The Somme was to prove a steep learning curve for the BEF which at the time comprised mainly volunteer or Pals battalions as well as a conscript force. This baptism of fire hardened the men to combat and the next series of battles featured a highly disciplined fighting force that was to prove effective in the decisive closing Allied campaigns of 1918. The irony was that these later campaigns are regarded as the most successful battles ever fought by the BEF under Haig's leadership.

The total British casualty figures for the Somme were close to 420,000 which included 127,000 dead and the rest wounded (most, permanently), captured or missing. And all this for the princely sum of seven miles of captured territory. The overall German losses were much higher and are conservatively estimated at more than 650,000 casualties, dead and wounded.The campaign lasted for five months until November 1916 and the final engagement was the Battle of Ancre at Beaumont Hamel, originally a 'day one' objective. The ultimate winner was the winter weather, which closed in bringing the campaign to a halt for both sides. This campaign more than any other in the war came to epitomise the waste of human life and was to wreak a particular devastation on the KSLI and its Shropshire contingent and in particular, the men of Wellington.

Somme Campaign (Part 2)
Personal Accounts of Wellington Servicemen
Private William Charles Phillips
(58th Battalion - Australian Imperial Force)

Two local Wellingtonians Colin and Gill Lewis relayed to me the story of their relative who was killed in the Great War, a costly battle described by Haig as 'a glorious sacrifice.' Colin has researched his

Colin and Gill Lewis with Private W.C. Phillips' medals

great uncle's contribution and even visited his war grave in France.

'My great uncle, William Charles Phillips was born in Wellington in 1895, son of William and Harriet Phillips.

In 1901 he lived in Arleston Village, Wellington, with his family comprising his brothers, John, Ernest and Norman and his sister Mary Annette.

Private W.C. Phillips - 58th Battalion and 5th Division, Australian Imperial Force

His half-sister Rhoda Shore lived with them as well, being the daughter of Harriet by a previous marriage. In 1909, tragedy struck the family when both parents died suddenly within months of each other and all of the siblings had to be split up. John lived with neighbours for a while and then joined the Royal Marines. Norman went to live in Coventry and Ernest went to live in Hadley a few miles away. Mary Annette was

W.C. Phillips' enlistment form

adopted by a couple in West Bromwich who later emigrated to Canada. Rhoda emigrated to Australia and when settled wrote to the boys asking them to join her but William was the only one who took up the offer to live with his sister. William enlisted into the Australian Imperial Force (AIF) on 23 July 1915 in Melbourne after answering the Commonwealth version of the famous Kitchener call to arms'.

Australia recruited 416,809 men and New Zealand had 120,099. Their combined force was known as the Australian and New Zealand Army Corps or ANZACS.

'He was 19-years-old and gave his occupation as cook.

On 28 January 1916 he sailed for Alexandria, Egypt arriving on 28 February.

Once there he underwent basic training. He was later transferred to join 1st Division Sanitary Section in Camp Zeitoun before going on to join 58th Battalion (58/AIF) in April 1916.

He boarded the troop ship HT Transylvania *on 17 June and arrived in Marseilles on June 23 for disembarkation.*

On 19 July 1916 he was killed in action during the Battle of Fromelles located 50 miles north west of the Somme. This was the first occasion that the AIF saw action on the Western Front and the force was virtually wiped out. William was buried the following day, 20 July, in the nearby military cemetery of Rue-du-Bois at Fleurbaix [Pheasant Wood] near Fromelles.

Rue-du-Bois cemetery at Fleurbaix, France

*His few personal belongings were sent back to his brother Ernest.
His army pension of nine shillings and sixpence per fortnight was paid
to his half sister Rhoda from 30 October 1916 to 15 April 1917 when
it was cancelled as she was deemed to be neither a blood relative nor
direct dependant.'*

The Battle of Fromelles: the Diversionary Feint
in the North That Wasn't

The Battle of Fromelles lasted from 19 to 20 July 1916 and was a
diversionary action by the Allies. It was designed to distract and pin
down key German divisions thus preventing them from supporting their
main forces, which were opposing the Somme campaign launched by
Field Marshal Sir Douglas Haig's Allied Forces (including the AIF).

It was fought under the command of Briton, General Richard
Haking, and took place some 80km (50m) north of the Somme and
involved a full-scale assault along a 6km front including an artificially
constructed fortified mound dubbed the Sugar Loaf.

Haking's battle plan was to rush past the first line of German

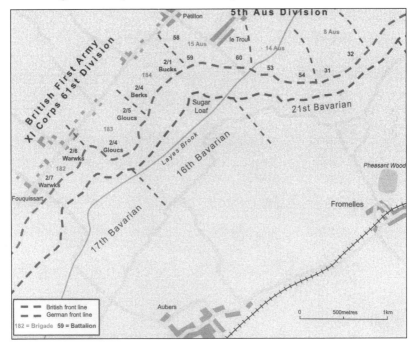

Fromelles battlefront map, 1916

trenches in a surprise attack during broad daylight after an initial artillery bombardment, and then advance 400 metres to a secondary line.This was an exceptional distance for the infantry to cover especially across the tortuous open ground of no man's land, which was exposed to murderous enemy gunfire.

The left flank of the battlefront was attacked by the 5th Australian Division AIF (which included William's 58/AIF) even though they had very little battle experience and were newly arrived in France. The British 61st Division (aka the 2nd South Midland Division) attacked the right flank. By the time the battle was launched the Germans had rumbled its purpose yet Haking was still keen to proceed although the advantage of surprise was now patently lost.

The main feature of this battleground was the Sugar Loaf fortified mound, so named by the Allies due to its distinctive shape. It afforded the holders (the 6th Bavarian Reserve Division) an advantage in allowing them to survey huge stretches of no man's land on either flank, comprising a flat featureless landscape as far as the eye could see. The Sugar Loaf itself was a concrete emplacement with several machine gun emplacements focused on all the gaps in the defensive line that the assaulting infantry would have to access.

The action began on 19 July during the evening after a seven-hour bombardment, that failed to displace the enemy positions and which the field artillery blamed on poor battlefield communications. Within the first few hours it became a bloodbath resulting in half the assembled AIF forces being wiped out, including William's 58th and elements of the 59th and 60th battalions.

It is debatable whether the action was necessary or even relevant strategically and is subsequently recognised as the biggest disaster to befall this colonial regiment. It is commemorated in the VC Corner, which is the largest dedicated Australian cemetery in France. The fighting was all over by 8.00 am, 20 July 1916 and resulted in 5543 Australian casualties with 1,299 killed and the rest either missing, captured or wounded.

It was regarded as being the worst 24 hours in Australia's history and the casualties were greater than those suffered in the Boer, Korean and Vietnamese wars put together. Brigadier General Harold 'Pompey' Elliott, commander of the 15th Brigade of the AIF (and William's overall commander) was, with his men, newly arrived in France in July 1916.

He was appalled to learn that his raw inexperienced recruits were to participate in a major engagement such as this.

It was customary with formations new to the Western Front to bed them in utilising a quiet corner, and Fromelles had seemed a relatively benign sector. So it came as quite a shock to Elliott to find his men were to join the 5th Division's imminent full-scale attack against the German line. The infantry went over the top at 6.00pm and the 8th and 14th brigades reached their initial objectives quickly. However, on reaching their secondary objective they found no viable means of sustaining their gains. The 15th Brigade (William's) and the British 184th Brigade were decimated by heavy machine gun fire while attempting to cross a narrower stretch closer to the German lines. A survivor, W.H 'Jimmy' Downing, Elliot's aide-de-camp later recalled: 'The air was thick with bullets, swishing in a flat, crisscrossed lattice of death. Hundreds were mown down in the flicker of an eyelid, like great rows of teeth

Brigadier General Harold Elliott, AIF, Commander in Chief

knocked from a comb.' The unfolding disaster was compounded when the 61st Division (BEF) asked the 15th Brigade (AIF) to support it in a renewed assault at 9.00pm but then cancelled its attack without informing the Australians. Consequently, the 58th Battalion (William's) made another futile attempt to capture the Sugar Loaf. The Germans succeeded in driving a wedge between the 14th and 15th brigades thus splitting the Australian forces. Isolated and outflanked, the 8th and 14th brigades were forced to withdraw the following morning. By this time the Germans had set up machine gun *enfilades* (crossfire) that caused devastating casualties amongst the retreating and disorganized AIF. As wounded Australians lay bleeding in no man's land, observers of the aftermath struggled for words. 'Most awful scene of slaughter imaginable', Downing said.

Other contemporary accounts include this observation from a 59th Battalion corporal, Hugh Knyvett.

'If you gathered the stock of a thousand butcher shops, cut into small pieces and strew it about, it would give you a faint conception of the shambles those trenches were.' Brigadier General Elliott greeted as many of the returning survivors as he could touring the line from battalion to company headquarters, shaking their hands and comforting wounded men.

Turning aside to one of his staff – Captain Trainer – he implored, with tears streaming down his face: 'Good God Bill, what have they done to my brigade?' Elliott lost a third of his men at Fromelles and the events would affect him deeply and permanently. He survived the war to form a successful legal firm but later committed suicide in 1931 which, it was agreed, was war-related.

It is reported that prior to the battle itself, which Elliott described as a 'tactical abortion', he had met with Major H.C.L Howard, a visiting staff officer from Field Marshal Haig's headquarters. Elliott took Howard not just to the frontline but to a forward observation post in no man's land that afforded a good view of the Sugar Loaf. Elliott showed the major his planned dispositions and draft orders and asked for his frank assessment of the outcome. Shocked at what he had seen on the ground, Howard admitted that the attack would prove disastrous. He further promised to go back to Sir Douglas Haig and tell him so personally. Whatever the result of this proposed discussion, the attack was not cancelled but only delayed. Thus the catastrophic engagement at Fromelles unfolded – advocated and orchestrated by BEF commander Haig – with no redeeming tactical advantages or justification whatsoever. It was a futile diversionary attack to try to pin down German forces in order to maximise the Allied effect on the main campaign of the Somme.

The Germans were not fooled, rumbling the tactic very early on and thereby negating any chance of a quick and decisive success by destroying the element of surprise.

After the war Rhoda tried to glean the circumstances of her half-brother's frontline death. She wrote a letter to the army records department in Australia requesting the details and the location of his grave

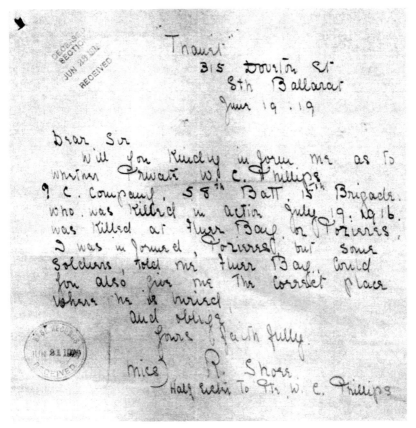

Rhoda's letter to the Army Records Office

The records office reply, dated 24 June 1919 and signed dutifully by the major in charge, was basic and said nothing more than William had died in France on19 July 1916 and it gave the location of his grave.

Colin and Gill Lewis have researched this battle extensively for reports detailing the exact circumstances of William's death but to no avail. They assume that due to the ferocity of the Germans' response to the initial assault, and the difficulty of the terrain, that he must have perished in this first wave of the 58/AIF that was in the centre of the attack and had taking the brunt of the casualties.

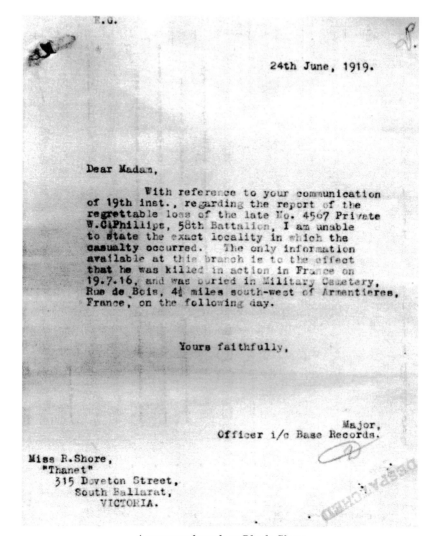

R.G.

24th June, 1919.

Dear Madam,

    With reference to your communication
of 19th inst., regarding the report of the
regrettable loss of the late No. 4567 Private
W.C.Phillips, 58th Battalion, I am unable
to state the exact locality in which the
casualty occurred. The only information
available at this branch is to the effect
that he was killed in action in France on
19.7.16, and was buried in Military Cemetery,
Rue de Bois, 4½ miles south-west of Armentieres,
France, on the following day.

        Yours faithfully,

                           Major,
      Officer i/c Base Records.

Miss R.Shore,
  "Thanet"
    315 Doveton Street,
      South Ballarat,
        VICTORIA.

Army records reply to Rhoda Shore

Somme Campaign (Part 3): personal accounts of Wellington servicemen

Of all the graphic accounts detailing the demise of Wellingtonians,
surely the most tragic involved the double loss suffered by this family.

Here, Joan Wedge of Dothill, Wellington recounts her maternal grandmothers' experiences in the war.

'As a fellow Wellingtonian, my granny Edith Emily Mansfield achieved notoriety as the holder of a unique and unenviable First World War record.

"Is this the unluckiest woman of the war?" blared the contemporary press reports.'

Apparently she had lost not just one but two husbands during the course of the war, leaving her a widow twice over with five children to raise all on her own. Both of her husbands are featured on the Wellington All Saints Church Lych Gate Memorial. The first was Samuel Harris who was killed during the Somme campaign at the Battle of Delville Wood, which also involved contingents of the South African Army. For clarity, here is an outline of the battle for Delville Wood in August 1916. It was nicknamed 'Devil's Wood' by Allied troops.

Mrs Edith Emily Mansfield

Delville Wood was one of the thornier objectives of the Somme campaign and comprised wooded hillocks that were home to oaks, hornbeam and beech trees covering 63 hectares. It proved difficult for

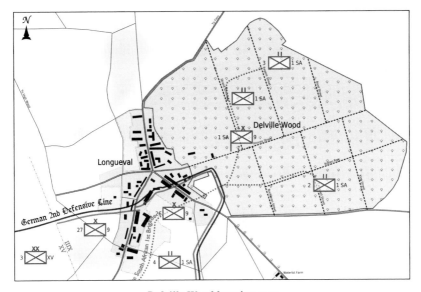

Delville Wood location map

Allied troops to dig in through knotty tree roots and was heavily fortified by the German field artillery. It would take several weeks to dislodge these forces in a counter attack that was to fall to troops from the Union of South Africa, then part of the British Empire. They lost 10,000 men in the process, over the course of an engagement that lasted from 14 July to 3 September. It was supported by elements of 5/KSLI in which Private Harris was serving. He met his death on 24 August 1916. His name appears on the Thiepval Memorial as well as on the main Wellington memorial, Lych Gate at All Saints Church. Private Harris is mentioned in the Wrekin District Roll of Honour biographies. The entry reads as follows:

17750 – Samuel Harris, 5th Battalion KSLI - Husband of Mrs E. Harris, Lewis's Passage, Park Street, Wellington. Killed in action in the battle of Delville Wood on the Somme, 24th August 1916. Having had 5 months training at Pembroke Dock he went to the front and had been there 15 months when he was fatally wounded. Previously worked at Haybridge steel works and Trench Iron works. Left a widow and 3 children. Aged 34.

Private Samuel Harris

Mrs Edith Emily Harris's suffering didn't end there. In 1916, she met and married another soldier who was ultimately to meet his fate in 1918 on the Western Front. Edith's granddaughter, Joan Wedge relates further.

'*Granny met another infantryman, Private George Herbert Mansfield in Wellington and married him, only to lose him also to this terrible war.*'

The Wrekin District Roll of Honour biographies also has an entry for Private Mansfield which reads as follows:

'*18746 – Private George Herbert Mansfield, 2nd Battalion*

Private G.H. Mansfield, 2nd Battalion, Royal Bedfordshire

Bedfordshire Regiment, Husband of Mrs Mansfield, 82 Park Street Wellington. Killed in action in France, 23rd October 1918, Aged 29. (Second husband of Mrs Mansfield whose first husband 17750 Private Samuel Harris was also killed in action leaving her with 4 young children).

The late Allied campaign that claimed the life of George Mansfield was the Battle of the Selle on 23 October 1918. It was the final Allied advance in Picardy and the regimental war diary for 2nd Battalion Royal Bedfordshire reads as follows:

23 Oct 1918: [the final advance in Picardy – the Battle of the Selle] – north east of Le Cateau-Cambrésis Battalion in Line. Operations N.E. of LE CATEAU. After a six-day halt for preparations and artillery bombardments Fourth Army troops attacked at 5.20am on Thursday 17 October; infantry and tanks, preceded by a creeping barrage, moved forward on a ten-mile wide front south of Le Cateau. The centre and

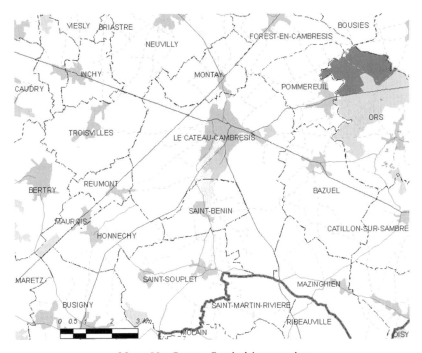

Map of Le Cateau-Cambrésis campaign

left of the Fourth Army forced crossings of the river despite unexpectedly strong German resistance and much uncut barbed wire. Fighting was particularly fierce along the line of the Le Cateau – Wassigny railway. The right of the attack, across the upland watershed of the Selle, made most progress and by nightfall enemy defences had been broken and Le Cateau captured. Severe fighting continued on 18 and 19 October, by which time Fourth Army, much assisted by the French First Army on its right, advanced over five miles, harrying the Germans back towards the Sambre-Oise Canal.'

The British Third and First armies, immediately to the north of Fourth Army, maintained the offensive pressure the following day. In a surprise joint night attack in the early morning of 20 October Third Army formations secured the high ground east of the Selle. Following a two day pause, to bring up heavy artillery, the attack was renewed on 23 October with a major combined assault by Fourth, Third and First Armies. The fighting continued into the next day and resulted in further advances. At this stage, the German Army retreated at a forced but controlled pace. On 24 October they counter-attacked at the Canal de la Dérivation but were repulsed and pushed back by the Belgian Army.

Medals and Awards of Service in the Great War

The highest end of the medals table did not distinguish between ranks. The Victoria Cross – the UK's highest award for bravery under enemy fire – was awarded to officers and other ranks without distinction. However the other awards were more discriminatory. An officer could win the Military Cross for conspicuous gallantry in the field but all other ranks (non-commissioned officer and below) were awarded Military Medal.

VC – Victoria Cross (all ranks)
MC – Military Cross (officers only)
MM – Military Medal (all other ranks)
DSO – Distinguished Service Order
DSM – Distinguished Service Medal
Croix De Guerre – France's highest award for bravery
               – won by British soldiers*
(*See Chapter 7 - Teece Roberts)

4 Star

The 1914-15 Star

The War Medal

The Victory Medal

1914 Star

and quite wrongly, called the 'Mons
he 1914 Star was issued to all officers,
en and women who were members of
the British or the Indian Expeditionary
including medical staff, who served in
or Flanders.

ugh members of the Royal Navy, Royal
s and of the various naval reserve units
ot eligible if they were on ship or at the
those who formed a part of shore-based
lid receive the star (these largely con-
with the actions around Antwerp).

cipients were required to have been on
ength of a qualifying unit and to have
ashore between August 5 and midnight
ber 22 - 23, 1914.

ited in April, 1917 initially as a star to be
n its own, on October 19, 1919, the King
ced the award of a bar to be sewn onto
on. The bar bears the inscription '5th Aug
Nov 1914' and denoted that the recipient
en under fire at the front between the
mentioned dates.

so-called 'Mons Star' was never intended
reward solely for those who fought during
eat from Mons, but rather to cover this
long with those at Le Cateau, the Marne,
ne, Langemarck, Gheluvelt and Nonne
en.

decoration was made in bronze as was
er bar. It was based on a simple four-
star, the upper-most point being blocked
a crown from which the suspension loop

nain design takes the form of two crossed
which pass through a wreath. A scroll
around the swords in three sections and
the inscription, from top to bottom,
'1914', 'NOV'. At the bottom of the
may be found the Royal Cipher 'GV' of
eorge the Fifth.

medal ribbon of equal stripes was red,
nd blue, shaded and watered. When worn
should be first with a silver rose denoting
if on undress uniform.

The 1914 - 15 Star

star could not be awarded to those who
held the 1914 Star, although it was
l for service not included within the above-
ed criteria (i.e. for naval personnel who
on a Royal Naval vessel rather than
. The service period ran up until midnight
ember 31, 1915.

personnel eligible included all officers,
officers NCOs and men of the British,
on, Indian, and Colonial Forces. These
number of doctors, nurses and por-
orking in overseas hospitals which were
ered to be within operational theatres of

fication as far as the Royal Navy was con-
service on board one of His Majesty's
vas required within areas regarded by the
ice as theatres of operation.

As well as the Royal Navy, the star could be
bestowed on members of the RNAS, RM, RNR,
RNVR and the RIM, as well as members of the
Dominion Naval Forces and their reserve forces,
along with non-naval/medical staff, and canteen
staff.

Personnel who served on the Indian Frontier
between November 28, 1914, and October 27,
1915, were eligible for this star as no bar was
issued to the Indian General Service Medal.

The design of the bronze star was almost identical to the 1914 Star with the exception of the
scroll which simply passed across the two
swords and bore the inscription '1914 - 15'.

The ribbon for the star was the same as the
1914 Star, although no bar or rose may be worn.

The 1914 - 20 War Medal

This medal was not approved by King George
the Fifth until 1919, although service in both Russia and in the theatres of the Russian Campaign
such as the Baltic and the Black Sea did qualify
as did mine clearance work at sea.

With the exception of the above mentioned
post-war qualifications all service had to be rendered between August 5, 1914 and November
11, 1918.

For members of the Army, the medal was
granted to all officers, warrant officers, NCOs
and men of the British, Dominion, Colonial, and
Indian Military Forces who had either entered a
theatre of the war under military orders, or who
had rendered service overseas.

Service in Ireland or at training camps on any
part of the then United Kingdom did not qualify.

The non-Army staff who qualified included
members of women's units working under the
auspices of one of His Majesty's Imperial Forces,
hospital staff serving in any theatre of the war,
certain labourers, colonial and non-colonial, acting as pioneers within a theatre of the war.

Members of the Royal Navy qualified for the
medal by performing at least 28 days service
within a theatre of the war, between the dates
given above for all branches of the armed services, while the next of kin received the medals of
those who were killed prior to the required accu-
mulated service.

In the case of naval personnel, the medal was
awarded to officers, petty officers, NCOs and
men of the Royal Navy, Royal Marines, Royal
Indian Marines, RNR, RNVR and to members of
the Dominion and Colonial Navy and their
reserves.

It may be noted that included among the RNR
recipients were those within the Trawler Section.

Those officers and men within the Mercantile
Marine were also given the medal as were members of the WRNS who served in the same theatres of operation, as did some of Queen
Alexandra's Nursing Service Reserve along with
other nursing staff, non-nursing staff, clerks, and
cooks.

The Royal Air Force had come into existence
on April 1, 1918 and was composed of the old
Royal Flying Corps and the Royal Navy Air Service.

The qualifying dates are the same as for the

Army, unless engaged in the war against the Bol-
sheviks.

The medal was open to all officers, warrant
officers, NCOs, men and women who made up
the Corps, including the Royal Air Force Medical
Service.

Under special circumstances the war medal
was issued to RAF, RFC and RNAS personnel
who had served in the United Kingdom.

Such exceptions were to pilots and aircrew
who had flown in combat over our shores or over
the Channel, pilots and aircrew who flew aircraft
to France as Ferry Pilots, and to those on the
early carriers and vessels transporting aircraft
across the sea to theatres of war were also
awarded the 1914 - 16 Medal.

The medal may be found issued alone if the
recipient did not serve in any areas which saw
any combat.

The medal was made of silver (bronze medals
being issued to 'native' recipients) and bore on
the one side a coinage portrait of King George
the Fifth along with the inscription 'GEORGIVS V
BRITT: OMN: REX ET IND: IMP:'.

The reverse represents St George on horseback holding a drawn sword and trampling a
skull and cross-bones and a shield bearing an
eagle.

In the background may be seen a risen sun
which was said to symbolise victory and a new
beginning.

The medal ribbon has a royal blue border while
the centre is orange with stripes of white and
black on either side. The medal hangs from a
plain bar which unlike those for most earlier campaign medals, did not swivel.

It may be noted that up until 1923 the possibility of issuing individual bars to the War Medal in
order to mark the various engagements which
the recipients took part was considered. However, the list ran into three figures and it was considered to be both impractical and too costly.

The Mercantile Marine Medal

This bronze medal was instituted in July, 1919,
as a reward for members of the British, Dominion, Colonial, and Indian Mercantile Marine.

Six months' service was required and the
medal was largely confined to fishermen and
ship's pilots, although the exact qualifying details
varied from country to country and in the case of
death due to enemy action the stipulated qualifi-
cation period was waived and the medal was
duly forwarded to the next-of-kin.

The 'heads' side of this medal is identical to
that of the War Medal, as is the type of suspension adopted.

The design chosen for the reverse was of a
merchant steamer which is shown in the fore-
ground, the background depicting a German 'U'
boat sinking and also a sailing vessel.

The ribbon represents the lights of a ship, red
for port, green for starboard, these being sepa-
rated by a central white stripe. The ribbon is seen
with the green first and foremost.

The Victory Medal

Made of gilded bronze, the Victory Medal was
instituted in 1920. The medal was made in the
light of the need for all of the allies to produce
some form of official award to recognise not only
service during the war but also the fact that such
service by individuals had led to the ultimate
victory.

Each of the nations embroiled in the World
War would produce their own medal which
would only be issued to their subjects, thus preventing mass duplication among the 20 or so
protagonists.

Eligibility for the Victory Medal is quite complex, this being essentially granted to all of those
who qualified for either the 1914 Star or the 1914
- 15 Star, or for the War or Mercantile Marine
Medal. Although it was possible for certain UK
and Colonial based personnel to hold only the
War Medal, the Victory Medal was never issued
singularly.

The design is of a winged figure of Victory
holding a laurel branch in her right hand and raising her left hand and her gaze to the skies.

The reverse bares a wreath within which are
the words 'THE GREAT WAR FOR CIVILIZA-
TION'. There is a lug at the top of the medal
through which a suspension ring passes. The ribbon is watered to give a rainbow effect viz. - red
in the middle, with green and violet stripes on
either side.

It was decided that an oak leaf should be worn
on the medal ribbon to denote a
mention-in-despatches.

Unlike the French Croix de Guerre, only one
bronze oak leaf was worn and there was no way
of distinguishing the level of bravery or number of
times that an individual had been 'mentioned'.

If the medal ribbon alone was worn, then a
smaller oak leaf was sewn across same.

The Territorial Forces War Medal

This medal was instituted in April 1920, to
reward members of the Territorial Forces who
had volunteered for overseas service prior to
October 1,1914.

Members were eligible if they had completed
four years service prior to the outbreak of the war
and had re-enlisted before the above mentioned
cut-off date, or who were members of the Territorial Force on August 4, 1914.

Although all recipients of the award had to
serve overseas the intention was to provide a
medal only for those who had not already qualified for the 1914 Star or 1914 - 15 Star.

The design of this bronze medal was similar to
that of the War Medal with a coinage head of the
King around which was the inscription 'GEOR-
GIVS V BRITT. OMN: REX ET IND: IMP:'. The
reverse bears a wreath, above which is the
inscription 'TERRITORIAL WAR MEDAL'.

Within the wreath itself may be found the
inscription 'FOR VOLUNTARY SERVICE OVER-
SEAS, 1914 - 19'.

The medal has a straight suspension, while the
ribbon is in a watered yellow with two equal
green stripes.

Medals and awards for servicemen

Servicemen's Award: The 'Death Penny' Memorial Plaque (Medallion)

The popular term 'dead man's penny' described a standard service award issued to the next of kin of all British and Empire personnel who served on the frontline. You only had to do one thing to receive it – die in battle. Measuring approximately 5 inches in diameter (120mm) and cast in bronze it was designed as the result of a competition, and was resplendent with the image of Britannia holding her trident, accompanied by a lion.

The design resembled the coinage at that time and the term 'death penny' came into usage as a metaphor for the appalling number awarded, due to the high casualty rates.

A total of 1,355,000 plaques were issued (even up to the 1930s) to commemorate those

*Croix De Guerre **medal***

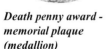

Death penny award - memorial plaque (medallion)

who died as a consequence of the war. The inscription around the face reads: He died for freedom and honour with the name of the recipient printed in capital letters inside a cartouche or rectangular box next to the figure of Britannia.

Provision of local hospitals set up to cope with battle casualties

Treatment facilities for Britain's war wounded were woefully in short supply at the beginning of the war so DORA empowered the War Office to requisition every available building deemed suitable for conversion or adaptation. Although fully equipped, these new military hospitals were run mainly for convalescing soldiers. Patients stayed for only three weeks on average as they were expected to recover quickly, regardless of the severity of their injuries, and return to the front as soon as possible.

The Wellington Cottage Hospital on Holyhead Road and the Wrekin building on the corner of Tan Bank and Walker Street were converted into surprisingly well-equipped hospitals.

Wrekin Hall YMCA Building

This facility was made available in Wellington as early as 1914 and thanks to the philanthropy of Mrs Dugdale and Lady Stafford it was converted into the Wellington Voluntary Hospital, as evidenced in the following *Journal* report:-

Wellington Voluntary Hospital

At the Wrekin Buildings, Wellington, by kind permission of Sir Charles S Henry Bart MP, Mrs Dugdale has fully equipped a hospital in readiness for wounded soldiers. Down to the smallest details the arrangements have been carried out in a most thorough and efficient manner. In the main hall there are 20 beds and by each bed a locker,

Wellington Voluntary Hospital Ward - first floor, Wrekin Building

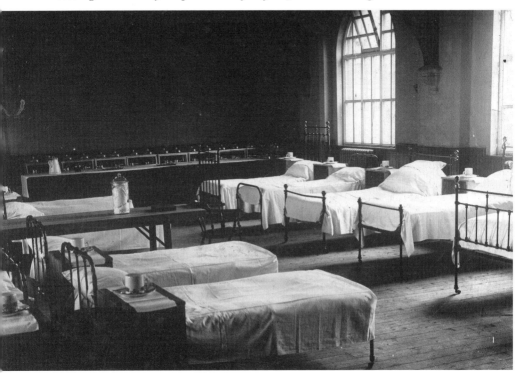

Wrekin (YMCA) building - modern exterior

together with necessary eating utensils. At one end of the hall there is a device by means of which the food of the inmates is kept warm during the time of dishing up meals etc – So all will be served at the same

VAD Nursing contingent - Wellington (A.F Print)

Nursing staff at Wellington Cottage Hospital, circa 1916

time with food of an equal temperature. It is in the smaller rooms, however where one sees with what thoroughness Mrs Dugdale has undertaken the equipment. Two large gas water-heaters, beautiful white porcelain sinks, ranks with all hospitals: operating rooms, isolation rooms, doctors rooms, and various other rooms make together with a staff of voluntary nurses, an institution which no doubt the army authorities will thoroughly appreciate.

Later in the war, as casualty rates increased, it was extended to 25 beds. The nursing was largely provided by a Voluntary Aid Detachment contingent .

Wellington Cottage Hospital

Wellington's other facility for the wounded serviceman was Wellington Cottage (later called Wrekin) Hospital. It was originally the infirmary of the union workhouse and also housed the town's mortuary. It was the only fully-equipped hospital available at the start of the war and it was soon converted into a military hospital.

Again it was supported by local philanthropists and business people such as a certain Captain G.A. Bosher – a partner in the steam haulage firm Bosher & Richards, based at 10 Park Street, Wellington.

Bosher is also featured in the patient group photograph taken around 1916 sporting his usual bushy moustache and wearing his broad-brimmed hat replete with feather. He was probably representing the Urban District Council in an official capacity.

It later operated as the local hospital before being absorbed into the NHS in 1948.

Captain G.A. Bosher (centre) - supporting a call for First World War volunteers

Wellington Cottage Hospital patients and Captain Bosher - centre of second row from the back

War Updates from the Somme 1916 – Extracts from *The Journal*

In the light of increasing censorship, newspapers were ordered to filter out bad news about the war.

Extracts from a report in *The Journal* dated 20 July 1916 read as follows:

The second phase of the offensive launched on Friday of last week has proceeded with great success. On Saturday at one point, the Germans were forced back to their third system of defences more than four miles their original trenches... . Sir D. Haig reported on Monday that the total of unwounded German prisoners taken by the British since the 1 July was: 189 officers and 10,779 other ranks... . Thus the allies had captured about 23,000 prisoners and 139 guns in total so far....

The British, the report continues, had gained important successes at three points.

North-west of Bazentin-le-Petit we took by storm; the second-line positions on a front of 1,500 yards; east of Longueval the gap in the German defences was still further widened by the capture of the strongly-defended Waterlet Farm, while the whole of the village of Ovillers where there had been hand to hand fighting since 7 July, was now in our hands... . Documents captured by the British showed the very heavy casualties suffered by the enemy in the recent fighting. One battalion had been reduced to three officers, two non-commissioned officers and 19 men... .

The King telegraphed to Sir D. Haig on Tuesday stating that the continued successful advance filled him with admiration – and he was sending best wishes to all ranks. The Tsar also congratulated the British troops upon the great success they have achieved... .'

Home Front

'In this war Britain is fighting three foes: The Germans, The Austrians and Drink - and drink is the one I fear the most'.
Prime Minister – (David Lloyd George, 1916)

How Wellington Managed its Home Front Defences

The concept of the Home Front was uniquely British, as other continental nations did not regiment their citizenry quite in the same way as the UK did.

Wellington's civic and public dignitaries organized the local community to prepare for invasion by rallying local support at meetings. This led to the formation of a local Volunteer Civilian Corps (VCC), or Home Guard comprising men (some of whom were ex-service men) ineligible for war service mainly because they were older. Their job was to protect the town in the event of foreign invasion. A few well-heeled businessmen and other private residents held a meeting in September 1914 and a committee was formed called the Wellington District War Assistance Committee. *The Journal* duly reported on its progress:

At a meeting of the Wellington District War Committee, which was held in Edgbaston House on Monday 31st August, 1914, it was suggested there were a number of men in Wellington and district unable to join Lord Kitchener's army either owing to age or business ties, etc., who felt they would like to get into a state of efficiency at this critical stage. With this in view a meeting was convened on the

J.A. McCrea - Battalion Quartermaster and 2nd Lieutenant Wellington VCC

Thursday evening at which it was decided to start a Civilian Corps for drill and rifle instruction. A large hall had been promised in the town for drill and it was proposed to obtain an efficient instructor. Only men who were not available for more active service will be permitted to join... .

And from a later report, dated 11 September: *A further meeting was held on Friday at the Grand Theatre, Tan Bank under the presidency of Mr G.H. Paddock * who explained that there were hundreds of capable men residing in that locality who were willing to serve their country but who were barred by age and other adverse conditions from going into the fighting ranks....*

On 14 November *The Journal* reported: *The formation of a Volunteer Civilian Corps for Wellington has been taken up with conspicuous enthusiasm and already some hundred recruits have been enrolled. These included all classes of the community. The Corps includes many old volunteers and ex-soldiers who showed remarkable agility on being put through their drilling evolutions and entered into them with enjoyable zest. A spokesman said that there will be preliminary drills held on Monday and Tuesday nights and later on would come route marches, rifle practice and general manoeuvres. Members of the National Reserve who were too old for National Service would also be eligible to join the Corps.. .*

The Journal on 30 January 1915 reported: *Mr J.A. McCrea, who was*

---

*G.H. Paddock was the father of Major H.L. Paddock who was killed in action. See Chapter 3.

appointed Hon. Secretary and Battalion Quartermaster, from March onwards will lead the Church Parade every Sunday in the role of 2nd Lieutenant of the Corps...

W Journal of 24 March reported that on Wednesday, the Civilian Corps was inspected in the grounds of Wellington College by Capt Sowerby assisted by Capt Dobson (Wellington College Officers Training Corps[OTC])... . And on 25 July, an interesting ceremony, hosted by John Bayley (Headmaster), took place at 3:30pm at the cricket pavillion in the college grounds when Lord and Lady Stafford in the company of Mr Beville Stanier, M.P. attended a special parade and distributed Brazzards (armbands) to over fifty members of the Wellington V.C.C. Under the command of Capt Sowerby assisted by Capt Dobson, the Corps were taken through a number of evolutions and the march past to the playing of the college OTC bugle band. The company then lined up in front of the pavillion where Mr Bayley briefly welcomed Lady Stafford. He said it could be thoroughly understood that the object of a Corps of that character was to fit in themselves that if, unfortunately, it should become necessary for them to play a part in the defence of their country, they would be quite ready to do it. The event was witnessed by a large concourse of spectators... .

Lord and Lady Stafford at Wellington College cricket pavillion

In October the Uniform Committee recommended wool serge caps and tunics, cotton Bedford cord breeches with putties (cost 37 shillings or £1.85) as the best and most serviceable all-year-round clothing. Rifles would be provided as they could afford them. The VCC appointed H.H. (Harry) Etches (senior clerk at Barber & Son, Wellington) as commander with the rank of senior lieutenant.

The Journal of 17 December 1915 reported that *A Colonel Leake, Commander of the Northern Battalion of Shropshire Volunteers, paid a visit to Wellington to inspect the Corps at the Gymnasium in Wellington College, where Capt Dobson addressed the assembled men. He said that members were now supplied with uniforms purchased at their own expense and have been instructed in musketry, bayonet and signalling work under Lieutenant Hammerton and NCOs at the College's Officer Training Corps.*

H.H. Etches, commander senior lieutenant, Wellington VCC

Wellington VCC contingent marching in the college grounds

It is debatable what contribution the VCC made to the security of the town but nevertheless they trained diligently and paraded regularly throughout the war.

Their model of honourable dedication and service in time of crisis helped establish the principle of the Home Guard in the Second World War which gave vital support to the nation.

Wellington's Boy Scouts and the Great War

It was the national call for wartime voluntary service that prompted Lord Baden-Powell, chief of the Scout movement, to issue a general command in telegram form as it was reported in *The Journal*.

The following telegram was received by Lord Harlech, Commissioner for Boy Scouts in Shropshire on Tuesday from General Sir Robert Baden Powell . 'Hope you can supply about 1000 scouts under District Commissioners to aid local civil or defence authorities in such duties as collecting or distributing information, re-supplies, billeting, guarding culverts and telegraphs, assisting post office, police, fire brigades, ambulance and poor relief distribution. War Office Informed) Baden Powell.' Lord Harlech expects that every scout in the county of Salop will do his utmost to carry out the wishes of the Chief Scout.

Group of Wellington Scouts, circa 1914

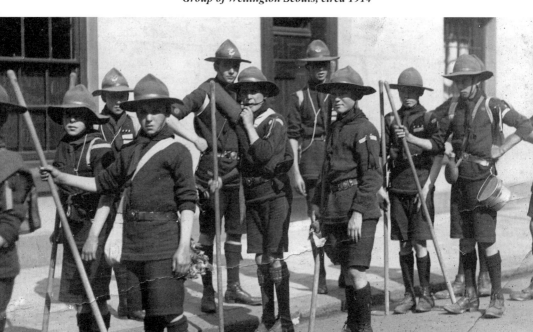

SHROPSHIRE BOY SCOUTS.

The following telegram was received by Lord Harlech, Commissioner of Boy Scouts in Shropshire, on Tuesday, from General Sir Robert Baden Powell:—"Hope you can supply about 1,000 Scouts under District Commissioners to aid local, civil, or defence authorities in such duties as collecting or distributing information re supplies, billeting, guarding culverts, and telegraphs, assisting post office, police, fire brigades, ambulance, and poor relief distribution. (War Office informed). Baden Powell."

Lord Harlech expects that every Scout in the county of Salop will do his utmost to carry out the wishes of the Chief Scout.

Shropshire Boy Scout - copy of original letter as reported in **The Journal**

General Sir Robert Baden-Powell, Chief Scout

This article challenged every Scout to do his bit for the Home Front in his local community. This consisted mainly of patrolling the local area on bicycles to observe and keep a lookout for any strange behaviour. Beyond these vague instructions the brief was sketchy and consequently not as effective or useful as it might have been.

Defence of the Realm Act: Wartime Effects on the UK and Wellington's Businesses

As wartime austerity bit into the national fabric of everyday life, the citizens of Wellington, in common with every person in the land, found themselves facing an array of enemies besides the Germans. One of the worst was their own government's wartime regulations. Within a few months of the outbreak, Asquith's government enacted DORA

AT THE COURT AT BUCKINGHAM PALACE,

The 1st day of September, 1914.

PRESENT :

THE KING'S MOST EXCELLENT MAJESTY IN COUNCIL.

Now, therefore, His Majesty is pleased, by and with the advice of His Privy Council, to order,

the following amendments be made in the Defence of the Realm Regulations, 1914:—

1. After Regulation 3 the following Regulations shall be inserted :—

"3A. The competent naval or military authority may by order authorise the use of land within such limits as may be specified in the order for the training of any part of His Majesty's naval or military forces ; and may by such

"3c. The competent naval or military authority may if he considers it necessary so to do for the purposes of any work of defence or other defended military work, or of any work for which it is deemed necessary in the interests of public safety or the defence of the Realm to afford military protection, stop up or divert any road or pathway over or adjoining the land on which such work is situate :

A sample extract of the list of DORA regulations, as reprinted in **The Journal**

under emergency powers legislation and this would have a profound effect on the lives of the British people.

This single piece of legislation was far more intrusive and imposing than any other restriction and its scope was unprecedented in English law. The Defence of the Realm Act 1914 – amended in 1915 – contained some harsh rules and regulations aimed largely at controlling its own populace and countering any perceived insurgency threat from foreign nationals residing in the UK.

This led to internment and vilification of all immigrants of German extraction and the willful destruction of their homes and businesses across the country, regardless of the contribution they had made to British society. Doctors, lawyers and academics were detained and in some cases not freed, until the end of the war.

As the war progressed the regulations became stiffer and so did the penalties. It seemed that the government was determined to interfere with and control every aspect of its citizens' lives. Businesses were also controlled closely under the Act so the beverages industry had its consumption, distribution and brewing methods altered.

Prior to the war licenced premises such as public houses were allowed to open at 5.00 am and close at 2.00 am. Under DORA and especially Lloyd George's administration these hours were reduced drastically. It was claimed that female munition workers were reporting for work in an intoxicated state thus putting their lives and the lives of their co-workers at serious risk. The opening hours were therefore reduced to 11.00 am to 2.00 pm and 6.00 pm to 10.00 pm, with greater restrictions on Sundays and these would remain in force until the 1980s. It didn't go down well with the average working man whose leisure time was restricted due to wartime work shift patterns. The seemingly harmless pursuit of drinking alcohol was viewed as a means

The Anchor Inn - Mill Bank, Wellington

to unwind from the daily grind and other worries. As consumption crashed, the entire alcohol industry – in particular the retail and brewing sectors (including the draymen who hauled the beer wagons) – was adversely affected in Wellington and throughout the country.

An early local casualty was The Anchor Inn in Mill Bank, Wellington, which had opened in 1828 and closed forever in 1916.

Other clauses in DORA allowed the government to commandeer buildings, assets and property for war use. This was demonstrated in Wellington with the arrival, early on in the war, of a convoy of motor vehicles. They were supplied by various northern businesses and parked in King Street, for a break, en route to military supply depots across the land.

Motor convoy parked in King Street en route to UK supply depots

Wellington Women in the War: Turning the Wheels of Industry

Female labour was relied upon to fill manpower gaps especially when conscription was introduced in March 1916.

This required all men between the ages of 18 and 45 to report for service in the armed forces. The need for women workers was especially pertinent in the munitions industry, which needed to be kept fully manned in order to keep up with demand from the War Office. Locally this situation affected the Sankey & Sons munitions works in nearby Hadley and the Lilleshall Company based in Coalbrookdale, Ironbridge.

Women in war munitions – Coalbrookdale, Ironbridge

The call went out to all local women, especially those from Wellington, and a great many responded. Across Britain, the number of women in manufacturing and engineering grew from 1400 in 1914 to over one million in 1918.

Single women in lodgings were seen as being particularly at risk from moral decay and had chaperones foisted on them in the guise of appointed wardens. These were usually older women who roamed at will to snoop on them and keep young men at bay. Many young female munition workers at the Lilleshall Company and women who lived in Wellington were affected by this snoopers' charter.

Wellington's Women Munitionettes: Personal Accounts

As women became part of the wartime industrial landscape terminology to describe their jobs crept into common usage. The female attendant on buses and trams was referred to as a 'clippie', a name that stuck after the war ended.

In the munitions industry the sudden appearance of women gave rise to the term 'munitionettes', which tended to glamourise their dangerous work and soften perceptions.

Wellingtonian David Barnett recalls his Great Aunt Alice (Barnett) and her friend Carrie Owen telling him how they did their bit for the war effort by working in a munitions factory in Morecambe, Lancashire. Women munitions workers were known as canary girls because the shell fillings, made from highly explosive TNT, coloured their skin yellow. The protective clothing provided was insufficient for such dangerous jobs and resulted in over 400 deaths from continuous contact with the poisonous material. David explains further: *'My aunt told us that The King [George V] and Queen [Mary] visited the White Lund munitions works in May 1917 and she had "a good view of them".'*

However, she must have been back in Wellington for the

Alice's notebook extract from 1918

Armistice in 1918 as this disapproving entry in her diary dated 12 November shows: *Armistice signed 11/11/18 – Some boys in Wellington that night. Good trade for drink. It was simply disgusting to see the folks rolling round the streets.*

Conscription and Wellington's Local Tribunals

Young men at home in Wellington and the surrounding area were summoned regularly to attend local tribunals convened to investigate why they had not as yet enlisted in the armed services. Some held

THE RECRUITING OFFICER, SHREWSBURY

Asks for information regarding the following men, as to whether they

(A) HAVE JOINED THE ARMY;

(B) ARE EXCEPTED FROM THE PROVISIONS OF THE MILITARY SERVICE ACTS, 1916;

(C) ARE IN POSSESSION OF A DEFINITE CERTIFICATE OR BADGE EXEMPTING THEM FROM LIABILITY FOR MILITARY SERVICE;

(D) ARE IN A RESERVED OCCUPATION;

(E) HAVE REMOVED TO ANOTHER DISTRICT.

Name.	Age.	Last Address.	Group or Military Service Act.
YETTON, LEONARD ERNEST	24	21, Barker Street, Shrewsbury.	Group.
ALLEN, JAMES	40	139, Frankwell, Shrewsbury.	M.S.A.
BRERETON, FREDK. CHAS.	31	Leighton Hall Remounts, Iron-Bridge, Salop.	"
DAVIES, HENRY	39	29, Claremont Hill, Shrewsbury.	"
EDWARDS, EDWIN	36	72, Castle Street, Oswestry.	"
EDWARDS, HOWARD	36	Broadway Farm, Ford's Heath.	"
FINNEY, HENRY	40	Frankwell, Shrewsbury.	"
GALLIGAN, EDWARD	36	138, Frankwell, Shrewsbury.	"
INGLIS, DANIEL,	31	24, Spring Gardens, Shrewsbury.	"
JONES, WALTER	27	Albrighton, Battlefield, Salop.	"
PRICE, EDWARD	35	1, Water Street, Castlefields, Shrewsbury.	"
PRICE, FRED	24	138, Frankwell, Shrewsbury.	"
PRICE, ISAAC	23	138, Frankwell, Shrewsbury.	"
RILLIE, JOHN	22	Newton Farm, Berwick, Salop.	"
RYAN, WILLIAM	22	Caravan, off St. Michael's St., Shrewsbury.	"
SALMON, JAMES WALTER	40	Remount Depot, Leighton Hall, Iron-Bridge.	"
SLATER, GEORGE	31	Harlscott Crossing, Shrewsbury.	"
SMITH, GEORGE	25	Model Lodging House, Frankwell, Shrewsbury.	"
SMITH, JAMES	39	c/o Mrs.G.Morgan, Preston Boats, Shrewsbury.	"
STEPHENS or STEVENS, WILLIAM	40	Frankwell, Shrewsbury.	"
SUTTON, ERNEST	30	Remount Depot, Leighton Hall, Iron-Bridge.	"
TAYLOR, HERBERT	29	Wharf House, Castle Foregate, Shrewsbury.	"
THOMAS, HERBERT GEO.	32	The Plox, Worthen, Salop.	"
CLARKE, FREDK. WM.	29	33, Corbett's Yard, Wellington.	Group
CAMDEN, CHARLES J.	35	24, Ladycroft, Wellington.	M.S.A.
WALTON, JOHN	23	Roden, Wellington.	"
HYDE, ALBERT GEORGE	25	Caledonia Hotel, Oakengates.	"
OWEN, THOMAS	29	4, Leonard Street, Oakengates.	"
MILLINGTON, ALBERT	38	70, Church Street, St. George's.	"
FITTON, GEORGE	40	50, Park Street, Wellington.	"
SMITH, HENRY	40	Ketley Brook, near Wellington.	"
PAGE, JOSEPH	40	The Old Windmill, Hadley, Salop.	"
SLADE, HENRY ROBERT HELGAR	34	Cleveland House, Wellington.	"
FINDON, THOMAS	33	c/o Mr. Chick, Sutton Maddock, Shifnal, Salop.	Group.
EGAN, THOMAS	36	12, Smithfield Rd., Much Wenlock, Salop.	M.S.A.
EVANS, ARTHUR	32	14, Brandley, Dawley.	"
MORGAN, EDWARD	30	84, Broadway, Shifnal.	"
MILES, JAMES WM.	27	15, Church Hill, Iron-Bridge.	"
CARLIE, WILLIAM	27	Acton Scott, Church Stretton.	"
OWEN, GEORGE	20	Swan and Falcon Hotel, Much Wenlock, Salop.	"

List of outstanding warrants for applicants not yet enlisted (extract taken from The Journal)

The above information is required to complete records in Recruiting Offices, and any communication will be treated in strict confidence.

Guildhall, Shrewsbury, 21/8/16.   H. R. S. COTTON, Major, R.O. 53rd Area.

legitimate paperwork as they were the only member of a family business left to keep it going. However, in cases of cancelled exemptions the business would fail and cause severe hardship.

Tribunals were often chaired by Mr A Lea Juckes, who apparently acted under the presumed authority of the Army yet held no official rank. He would enforce the rules stringently. Pleas of mitigation from service due to family, exempted, reserved occupations or the protection of business interests were largely ignored.

Late or missing attendees were dealt with summarily and warrants were issued for their arrest, detention and immediate dispatch to Army enlistment camps.

Several local firms were affected such as Groom's timber yard which should have had a staff of over 50 skilled workmen but was reduced to 18, plus five office staff despite having to fulfil government contracts. Letters from the Controller of Supplies pleading that the men held reserved occupation status (and thus war service exemption) were produced as evidence at tribunals but to no avail. It seemed Mr Lea Juckes would rather see local businesses destroyed than let one man evade military service.

Sir John Bayley forms the Officers' Training Corps at Wellington College

Due to the rapid expansion of the Army by volunteer enlistment and the ever-increasing casualties there was a critical shortage of experienced officers.

The shortfall was made up from the OTC, which was modelled on the procedures and training of the Regular Army. These were formed at public schools and colleges across the land including Wellington College.

John Bayley had opened the college as a private school in 1875. It soon gained college status and established his reputation as an innovative educationalist, which would lead eventually to a knighthood and national fame.

In 1909 Bayley was determined to form an Officers' Training Corps (OTC) at Wellington College but to do so, he needed authorisation from the Education Department in Whitehall, London.

WELLINGTON (URBAN).

Mr. J. F. Robinson presided on Tuesday.—Mr. R. A. Newill, representing the employer of the Wellington town missionary, who had been refused exemption by the Tribunal at a previous meeting, asked for permission to appeal on the employer's behalf, and stated that it was under a misapprehension that he did not apply for exemption for him before. He had now been called up, and having regard to all the circumstances his employer desired him to remain in the useful position he at present occupied. His duties had already been fully disclosed. The matter had been discussed by the Advisory Committee, and he (Mr. Newill) understood that they felt that the missionary should have the right of appeal. He was 41 years of age last August.—It was agreed that leave of appeal be given.——An ironmonger (represented by Mr. R. Gwynne) applied for further exemption for his manager and accountant, 29, single, and in Class C1. Mr. Gwynne stated that the employer was in his 76th year, and was unable to superintend the extensive business in such a way as a younger man would be expected to do. It had been established for 50 years. The employer's only son had been given to the army, and nearly everyone of his other eligible men had been taken, the result being that practically the management of the whole concern depended upon the man for whom application was now being made.—Mr. A. L. Juckes (military representative) said he thought that three months' final exemption would be quite sufficient in this case, as the man had been passed in a class which at present was badly wanted in the army. Had (he asked) any serious attempts been made to replace the man?—Mr. Gwynne: Yes; but without the slightest result. Every effort has been made. Allowed till July 10.—There was a military appeal against a solicitor's clerk, 30, married, C3, and Mr. Juckes asked for a removal of the exemption certificate and an order for re-examination by the medical board.—The Tribunal agreed to the re-examination, and for the case to be brought forward again.—Mr. J. V. Lander represented a firm of Government contractors engaged in woodwork, and applied for exemption for an accountant and estimate clerk, 36, married (with five children), A.—The firm's manager said that 90 per cent. of what they were at present doing was Government work, and their staff had been reduced to its utmost minimum if this work was to be completed.—Allowed till July 10, the man to continue with the V.T.C.—Application was made for extended exemption for an assistant-sawyer, employed on Lord Barnard's estate, and who is also a licensee. It was stated that the man put in full time; but, having heard the rate of wages paid, Mr. Juckes said they did not suggest that the man was engaged in a skilled occupation. It occurred to him that sometimes advantage might be taken of a man's conditional exemption by offering him low wages to follow civil employment, and if it were not for the war men would not be willing to accept such low wages. Allowed till July 10 on the man's application only, the employers' application being refused.—A firm of agricultural implement dealers applied for a fitter and mechanic, 29, married, who had not yet been medically examined, and who was stated to be an expert with various kinds of engines and machinery erection and repairs. Under existing conditions it would be impossible to replace him. No previous application had been made for exemption for him. Allowed till July 10, the certificate not ...

WELLINGTON (URBAN).

Mr. E. T. Morgan presided on Tuesday.—The Military Representative (Mr. A. Lea Juckes) referred to the conditions imposed by the Tribunal that when exemptions are granted the men should drill with the Shropshire Volunteer Regiment and become efficient. He stated that the record of attendances was in many cases unsatisfactory, and where the conditions were not complied with he should ask in future that the men concerned be written to, and if there was no improvement he should ask that the certificates of exemption be cancelled forthwith. To become efficient it was necessary for men to put in at least 14 drills a month, out of a possible 29, and he understood that the arrangements were such that the number of attendances could be made without any serious difficulty arising. A drill for two hours on a Friday counted for two attendances, and the same number were allowed for the Sunday drill of two hours. Therefore even that number would mean 16 drills a month. He hoped employers would assist in the matter, and point out to their workmen who are retained that it was essential that they should become efficient Volunteers.—A fish and game dealer, married, C1, applied for a renewal of his exemption certificate. The Military Representative stated that the attendances of this man at drill were very satisfactory. The man had a business, was doing his duty as a Volunteer, and had become a non-commissioned officer. Temporary exemption for six months was granted, the man to continue a member of the Volunteer Regiment. — An application was made by a clerk, who is also relieving officer, for the removal of the condition of his exemption that he drill with the Volunteers. Applicant explained the nature of his work, showing that he was engaged on important duties every evening. The Tribunal decided to remove the condition in this case.—A commissioned officer in the Volunteers, a fully-qualified chemist, was granted conditional exemption, being in a certified occupation.—Conditional exemption was also given to a clerk in the commercial department of a newspaper office, married, C3.—A motor-assembler, married (41), C1, applied for further exemption. The employer stated that if the man were called up for military service it would seriously interfere with the business. The Military Representative pointed out that one man, not a skilled workman, could not have such a serious effect on a business which was chiefly that of doing repairs. Exemption to Oct. 16 was granted.—The application for a branch manager of an insurance company, married, C3, was next dealt with. It was stated that the company had released a large number of men for the Army, and only desired to retain those of a low medical category. The Military Representative said the man was required as a clerk. Application refused.—An application for re-hearing was made in the case of a butcher's manager, who had been called up for August 1. The application was refused, with a recommendation to the military that a few days' extension be given if found necessary. — A butcher's horseman, married, C2, was granted further exemption, on the application of the employer to Oct. 16.—A relieving officer for Wellington Board of Guardians, married, B3, was granted six months' exemption on the condition that he joined and became an efficient member of the Volunteer Regiment.—A single man, a printer, was also granted six months' exemption; to become an efficient Volunteer.—An employer asked for a renewal of exemption for a motor-mechanic. It was pointed out that the man and other workmen had not put in the requisite number of drills with the Volunteers, and the employer undertook to see that an improvement was made. Temporary exemption until Oct. 16 was given, the man to become an efficient Volunteer.—A saddler, B1, married, was given six months' exemption; to drill with the Volunteers. The man stated that he would do all he could to assist in the Volunteer movement; but at present he was working seven days a week.

Examples of Juckes' tribunal cases as printed in **The Journal**

Sir John Bayley

His request was initially refused but due to his dogged persistence, permission was eventually granted and he formed his first company, which soon expanded to a second company. He established the course at the college as part of the curriculum and attracted fee-paying families who wanted to ensure that their sons were properly educated and

OTC band - church parade, Wellington

brought up in the 'proud traditions of British military discipline' as quoted in the college prospectus of the time. In the summer of 1911 the *War Office Times and Naval Review* published a series of pamphlets entitled *The Selection of a School.* One of these was devoted to Wellington College and its principal John Bayley. The praise heaped upon him is lavish indeed: *An experienced educationalist, Mr Bayley has probably spent more money in establishing a great school than any other teacher in the country. He has had a very wide experience of businessmen and has visited works and schools of every kind in Germany, France and Switzerland, so that he is well acquainted with all those ideals of school and business life which so eminently fit him to deal with the boys and young men committed to his charge.*

The OTC at Wellington College was fully inaugurated in 1912 and was featured leading the Sunday morning church parade along Church Street to All Saints Church on Church Green.

In anticipation of weapons training, Bayley had built a practice

OTC church parade. It had its own uniform and was later equipped with rifles through the War Department, supplied via the KSLI

Wellington College shooting range

shooting range at the college in 1909. In later years this facility would be used by the Civil Defence Corps for training.

It was not long before the OTC was called upon to support the BEF in France, which by 1916 had lost an appalling number of officers as well as soldiers.

Those that were ready trained and drilled leapt straight to the front of the recruiting queue. As officer shortages became more acute, the OTC's sacrifice became greater. It is a sobering thought to note that they lost sixty old boys in the war of whom half were OTC junior officers.

After the war the chapel in the grounds of Wellington College was dedicated to their fallen.

The total number of 'old Wrekinians' (Wellington College old boys) who took part in the First World War is 336 which meant around one in six died. A survey of the ages of those who lost their lives shows that seven were under twenty years of age, twenty-eight were aged twenty to thirty and nine were aged over thirty.

One of those whose name is on the college and Lych Gate Memorial is Lieutenant A.E.S.(Stuart) Hodgson. He was Wellington College's most famous old boy, his service on the frontline was exemplary, and his death was to affect the founder in a very personal way.

Memorial chapel Wellington/Wrekin College

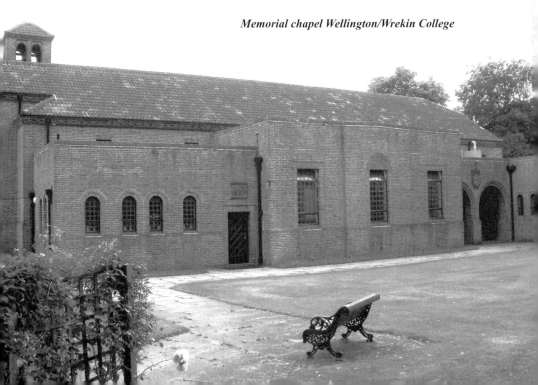

OTC graduation class lineup 1917 prior to embarkation and mostly killed in action

Stuart was the son of Marion Hodgson who was housekeeper to John Bayley from 1901. Consequently Stuart had lived within the Bayley household from the age of three. He was a pupil in the college but left at age 16 in September 1914 when he started training at an electrical works in Wolverhampton with the intention of going to Birmingham University two years later. However as he looked older than he was, people thought he had avoided enlisting and he was being handed white feathers, which were a sign of cowardice.

This was a common practice adopted by organized gangs of young women across the UK who would tour the streets and seek to publicly intimidate any young man who was not wearing a uniform. This was a political trade-off organized by the Women's Social and Political Union (WSPU) under the leadership of Emmeline Pankhurst.

The WSPU agreed to suspend violent suffragette activities during their campaign for women's voting rights for the promise of emancipation once the war was over. In return they would support the war with equal vigour and organized local women.

Lieutenant. A.E.S. Hodgson
from Bayley's OTC

False accusations occurred when their zeal overcame their virtue and they accosted men who weren't in uniform, even when they had a legitimate reason for not being in the services. This was the case with Stuart Hodgson who was technically ineligible to serve because he was underage. Nevertheless he decided that he would enlist and do his bit in the Army. Jonas Hammerton, deputy to John Bayley, obtained papers for him to enrol in the York and Lancaster Regiment. Stuart completed the papers but did not give his age and did not include his birth certificate. He was called for interview at Roker in Sunderland and the presiding colonel never asked his age.

On hearing he had two years' experience with the OTC, the colonel said: 'We want young fellows like you who have done some training.' His commission came through a week later with orders to report to Roker in two weeks. He was attached to the 3rd Battalion as a second lieutenant in April 1915 at the age of sixteen and a half. He went to France just after his seventeenth birthday in September 1915 and served in the Ypres battle of that winter. In a letter home he described his early experiences:

'We have just come out of the trenches, having had six days in. We have been fairly lucky this time and have not had a great number of casualties. I must say I felt a bit queer when I saw the first man fall. The trenches are so bad now that we keep moving about every two

days. Some naturally are much worse than others, and we went into some where the water was right up to the waist. We are fitted with gum boots reaching to the thigh, but even then we often get very wet. The winter is now coming into greater prominence. We have had several hail storms and every night there is a heavy frost, which makes things rather unpleasant to work. As you know, we work all night and try to sleep by day.'

He was wounded and invalided home. While recuperating he did some service with the regiment in Sunderland before returning to France in September 1916. He was killed in the Somme campaign, on 12 October 1916, a few weeks after his 18th birthday. His body was never recovered and his name is recorded on the Thiepval Memorial (Pier 14, Face B) amongst over 70,000 others who have no known grave. News of her only son's death reached Marion Hodgson whilst she was working in the Voluntary Auxiliary Hospital. This had just been established in the college using College House and Bayley's recently vacated house, Newlands, to provide nursing care for up to 25 wounded soldiers.

Mrs. Hodgson was acting as a liaison between the college and the military staff. She continued to act as housekeeper to John Bayley until

Newlands House at Wellington College, circa 1916

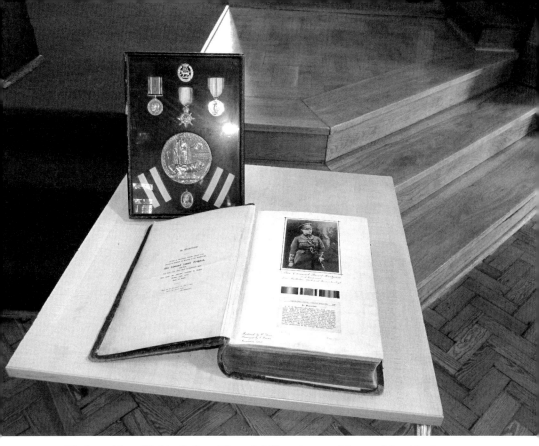

Display table at Wrekin College Memorial Chapel, comprising medals with photo of Stuart Hodgson and his mother's memorial bible

he sold the college in 1920 and it later became Wrekin College. She kept contact with him for many years and returned to present a copy of the 1613 King James Bible to the chapel as a memorial to Stuart.

The bible contains copies of letters and documents from which these notes were compiled. There is also a framed collection of the medals, badges and other memorabilia relating to her son, together with his service medals and his 'Death Penny'. John Bayley paid tribute to Stuart Hodgson in the *Wellington College Magazine*:

My young friend, Sec.-Lieut. Stuart Hodgson, 3rd. Batt, 2nd York and Lancaster Regiment, who has lived with me since he was three years of age, was killed in action on the Somme, October 12th 1916. This brave lad felt it to be his duty to his country to join the Forces and his equally brave mother raised no objection when he presented himself at Headquarters and took a Commission at sixteen and a half years of age. His was one of the grim Battalions which held the infernal Ypres salient through the awful winter of 1915-16, during which Lieut.

Hodgson and another officer were given a most valuable map of the German Trenches and Machine Guns. Soon afterwards he was invalided home, and for a time undertook work of Captain's rank at Sunderland and Newcastle. In due course he returned to the Front, and in a bold attempt to make it easier for his men to advance, he made the 'great sacrifice'. He is reported by those who worked by his side as one of the cheeriest and most encouraging of young officers, that he hardly knew what fear meant, and was a great credit to the Regiment to which he was attached. In our School, in our Country and Empire, let us give eternal honour to all these young souls who like my 'young charge' have nobly fought and nobly died that we might live. All 'old boys' and parents who remember Mrs. Hodgson will join with the whole School in tendering to her our heart-felt sympathy in the loss of her only son, but we would ask her in this hour of grief and sorrow, to try to share our feelings of pride in the great sacrifice she has made. Mothers and sons are giving their best in the service of God and Humanity. We hate War, but we prefer War rather than Liberty and Civilisation should be crushed under the heel of Prussian militarism, and if in this titanic struggle, our brave young heroes die at the post of duty we may take comfort in the words of the poet John Oxenham: Whether they live or die, Safely they'll rest; Every true one of them, Thy Chosen Guest. No soul of them shall fail, Whate'er the past; Who dies for Thee and Thine, Wins Thee at last.

So my brave young friend Stuart, on the battlefield of France we leave thee, peacefully asleep not far from many of thine old schoolfellows, and to all of you our last words are: Farewell! Farewell! Until we meet, as we shall meet, again.

Wellington's Other Public Schools in the Great War

As well as Wellington College, other local public schools also gave their best blood to the conflict – such as the Old Hall School, Wellington.

The Headmaster at the time, Ralph Hodgson Hickson (head of the school 1906-1926) would record in the school newspaper the progress of the war, news of their old boys' exploits and in which theatre of war they were fighting.

Old Hall School's Great War memorial tiled wall plaque

The excitement and dedication with which Hodgson Hickson publicised these facts continued for the duration of the war. It chimed with the prevailing national attitude that they were fighting a just and courageous war against an oppressive enemy.

In 1917 Captain Lascelles, father of one of the boys, was awarded the Victoria Cross to add to his Military Cross and the school celebrated with a half-day holiday. This was tinged with sadness when Lord Forester, a friend and supporter of the school, died the same year. The number of the fallen reached eight, when Aden Mason of the Staffordshire Yeomanry was killed in Palestine, aged twenty-three, on 19 October 1918. Parents and Staff clubbed together after the war to raise the commemorative war plaques we see today.

Local War News - as Reported in *The Journal*

The Boys' High School in King Street (now New College) had followed Wellington College's lead and set up its own Cadet Corps.

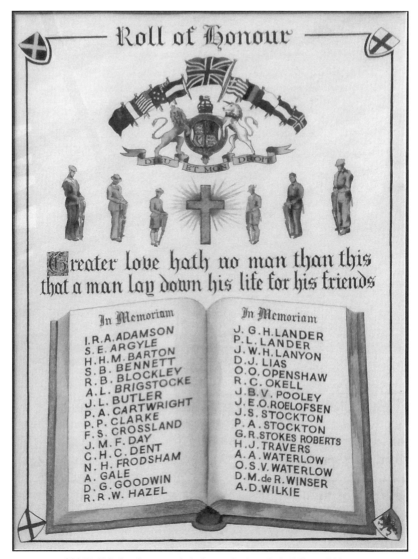

Old Hall School: memorial plaque listing their fallen old boys

The Journal reported: *With the annual inspection of the Corps by the Staffordshire Territorial Force Association on Monday was combined the competition for the Lucas-Tooth prize, and medals, for which the Corps was asked to enter. The Inspecting officers were Col. Cholmondeley, CB, and Capt. Sir Beville Stanier MP, accompanied by Capt. Maitland. 46 members of the Cadet Corps and Capt. H.W Male (Head) paraded.*

Stalemate

Dire Warnings of Catastrophes and Deadlocked Campaigns

By April 1917 Haig and the Allies knew they had to break the deadlock and take the fight to the enemy. His plan involved a campaign to take back the ground at Ypres, scene of the narrow Allied victory in 1915 and subsequently recaptured by the Germans.

It was now a rush to take back ground in north-west Belgium and recapture the coastal ports to outflank the Germans and thereby stem the submarine attacks on shipping.

The *Kaiserheer* had been fighting in this salient since 1914 and although the Allies had been successful once, they were repulsed in every later campaign.

What was to be called the Battle of Passchendaele (Third Battle of Ypres) began in July 1917 and was again initially successful for the Allies. But as the autumn bled into winter and German resistance remained strong, the Allies came to rely on their field artillery to decimate the landscape. The terrain turned into a quagmire that favoured neither side and the operation degenerated into another battle in a long war of attrition.

Passchendaele Ridge, Ypres battle scene, 1917

Haig was to be further vilified for prolonging rather than suspending the battle, given the conditions and thus causing the needless mass slaughter that occurred. The Allied losses far exceeded the strategic value of the ground gained, resulting in over 325,000 casualties.

Lloyd George had argued against the campaign along with Marshal Ferdinand Foch of France. Haig's standing had much declined after the failure of the Nivelle Offensive on the Western Front in April 1917 and Lloyd George had insisted that Haig be put under the command of Marshal Joffre. German casualties are estimated at 260,000 (killed, wounded and missing) over the period up to November when they were overrun and the position secured by the Allies.

Although the Germans were caught on the back foot it was to prove a cathartic experience for their strategic planning. General Erich Frederich Wilhelm Ludendorff would begin his campaign planning for the following spring with the fervent intention to keep the fighting mobile and not trenchbound as before.

Ludendorff was second in command only to Paul von Hindenburg Field Marshal and commander of all German land forces and was virtually the sole dictator of strategy for the German forces. Kaiser Wilhelm had become a remote figure taking no part in the day to day conduct of the war. An all out assault was needed for early spring 1918 to dissipate the current Allied strength and force an early negotiated truce with honour before the Americans could arrive to overcome them and win by sheer weight of numbers. This would effectively remove the option of a negotiated peace and replace it with the prospect of Germany having to concede defeat. Another spectre loomed on the horizon for the Germans (and for the Allies if the truth be told) in the shape of shortages. Lack of basic commodities was beginning to affect both sides' capacity to wage war for very much longer.

Rationing Nationally and Locally

Although an economic powerhouse at the time of the Great War, Britain relied heavily on foreign goods to supply itself with food and raw materials, and imports accounted for over one-third of its national requirements. Plundering the colonies for raw materials was fine in peacetime but as war commenced and naval blockades became standard operational practice, the shortfalls of basic essentials were felt almost immediately.

Shortages of beef products and also nitrates (needed for fertilisers and explosives) from South America began to affect food production. The wartime priority became the supply of the munitions industry rather than maintaining or increasing food output.

At the other end of the supply chain, farmers were complaining that crops were rotting in the field for want of harvesting. The industry had very few machines and was still highly labour intensive. As farm workers were mostly in the King's uniform, manpower on the land began to reach critical levels. In 1917 the Women's Land Army was founded and organized by Meriel Talbot, who had been appointed the first woman inspector for the Ministry of Agriculture the previous year. In response to a national advertising campaign thousands of women signed up and were given six weeks initial training at selected farms to get them used to handling equipment and livestock.

Although farm work was notoriously low paid, many girls were tempted away from much higher-paying munitions because they wanted to work in a healthier environment. By 1919 their ranks had swelled to 23,000. Even after the war ended, they were still needed.

In the UK, shortages of food and fuel became more of a problem even after the initial panic-buying had subsided. Steps were taken by

Women's Land Army poster
(Imperial War Museum)

the government to limit the sale of petrol for cars (then viewed as luxuries) and to reduce the price of household gas.

Prices for other basic fuels, such as coal for domestic use, had an upper limit imposed.

The Wellington Food Committee acted quickly, opening up sites (such as the grounds of the Boys' High School in King Street) for use as allotments to encourage residents to grow their own fruit and vegetables. Being at the heart of a farming community, supplies such as meat were plentiful in Wellington. However, with rationing in place, the council thought it necessary to place bogus orders with local butchers to gauge the extent of black market activity: reassuringly not one took the bait. Turkeys, pheasants and rabbits were keenly sought after and farmers took advantage of high prices. At nearby Eyton Pools, pike and other fish were fished to near extinction. Other commodities such as pork, milk, butter and margarine were in short supply and occasionally police were called to supervise disorderly queues. In 1917, the Salop Agricultural Committee stated that 'food shortages were enormous and menacing and England was fast declining in productive power.' Flour supplies eventually ran short, affecting bread production and forcing some local bakeries to close or move to another town. Private pig keepers risked prosecution for hoarding hams and bacon 'to the detriment of fixed prices' decreed by government.

Letters Home From the Trenches by Wellington Men

Sergeant Thomas Albert Powis 17118, 7/KSLI

Mrs Angela McClements, the great niece of Sergeant T.A. Powis explains how the letters he wrote home helped clarify what life was

Sergeant T.A. Powis, 7/KSLI

like on the frontline. The letters received from his fellow soldiers and Army staff, explain how he came to meet his death and where he is laid to rest.

I never knew my Great Uncle Thomas but my favourite aunts, Dorothy and Lilian, had always regaled me with stories of his involvement in something they called the Battle of Polygon Wood in Belgium.

From the tender age of seven my aunties told me of his bravery in trying to capture an enemy position when he was killed. This was all part of my family's memories of a brave 'great' uncle who served in the Great War.

Great Uncle Tom's family home was 54 Ladycroft, Wellington and he was the son of Edith and Robert Powis. He was brother to Lilian, Elsie, Robert (Bob), Dorothy, Florence, Benjamin (Dick), Reginald and Joyce.

He had previously worked at the CWS (Co-operative Wholesale Society, now known as the Co-op) at Wellington, Oakengates and became Assistant Manager at the Trench branch in Wellington.

He enlisted locally in 1915 at the age of eighteen and after initial training at Pembroke was sent to the non-commissioned officer (NCO) training centre at Oswestry.

Great Uncle Tom has been in my memory since I was a very young child. My great aunts, Dorothy (Dotty) and Lilian (Lily) always used to talk about their brother Tom. They were so proud of him and used to tell me stories of how brave he was and the battle 'across the sea' that led to his death. I knew nothing then about the battle he fought in, or the history surrounding it. It was only in later years, when I researched the narrative around their stories and read the letters written by friends and officers after he died that I began to understand what really happened. Then it all started to make sense.

Probably the earliest recollection I had of my Great Uncle Tom was when I was about 7-years-old in 1965. I can remember my (Great) Aunty Lily and (Great) Aunty Dotty showing me his name on the Lych Gate Memorial in Wellington and I thought then that he must be a very,

very special person. They told me stories about him being killed in a battle which involved a pill box and he got so close he could see the German soldiers. Not fully understanding what a pill box was, all I could visualise was a post box and therefore couldn't understand why there would be a battle to try and capture a post box.

He was actually killed by sniper fire at the Battle of Polygon Wood on 26 September 1917 and was within a few feet of a German concrete pill box.

His letters home are so endearing, always asking about how the family were, never moaning and never ever giving away what it must have been like for them on the frontline. There is only one letter that mentions "mud, mud everywhere".

It's only in recent years that we've known the full truth of the terrible and horrific conditions and I can begin to understand what he must have been going through. He dealt with it with such strength of mind and dignity.

In April of this year [2014], I travelled to Belgium and was fortunate enough to visit Tyne Cot Cemetery. It was quite an emotional moment seeing his name on one of the white stone plaques and seeing the names of all the comrades who fought alongside him in the KSLI. Sadly, it looks as though he doesn't have a grave. Reading through the letters from one of his soldier friends, it said he was probably buried by the Australians – I would like to think so. But one thing is sure, Thomas Albert Powis will never be forgotten by his family and his memory lives on to another generation.

Below are two of his letters that offer a flavour of life in the trenches away from home and family. Sometimes perhaps written under stress or in the quiet moments between battle campaigns. They are reproduced by kind permission of the McClements family.

First Letter from Tom Powis

Sent from the trenches on the Western Front in France, dated 14 May 1917:

Dear Mother & Dad

I have not any dought [doubt] *but that the letter mentioned in the note which came with the parcel is on the road, not having received it up to the date of writing, I think it is time I sent you a line or so, besides the whizz bang [soldier's postcard] posted about a week ago. The parcel I received in good condition together with the note. Dear Mother, the weather now being quite warm, I don't think it necessary for you to send any more abs* [ablutions kit]. *Soap in every other parcel will be quite sufficient The home-made cake of yours always goes down well, at least some of the boys say so. I have written to aunt Molly several times & have replies saying that they are all quite well. Dick is in some camp near Liverpool, I have had a letter from him saying that if he ever comes to France again he hopes to see me. I hope that he will not leave the shore of the good old mother country again, let alone come out here to scrap. It is fine weather in which to do the latter in, but the atmosphere gets too warm at times. Still, I suppose 'old fruit'* [Family endearment] *has to do it. I think it must be rather hot for huns* [Germans] *sometimes when our artillery fires out at them again - we're winning easily (I ought to be home soon, at least so the papers say). So cheer up there's hope yet.*

I do hope that Lil is getting on fine now, should like to see her so as to be able to form an opinion as to that. I suppose all the kiddies are alright and Bob is getting on with that job of his fine. You will give my best wishes to the neighbours around you. Well I hope these few lines of scrawl will find you all in the best of health, which applies to me at present. Now coming to a close with the best of love to all. Your loving son Tom XXXXXXXXXXXXX

Second Letter from Tom Powis

Sent from the trenches on the Western Front in France, dated 12 September 1917:

Dear Mother,

I have not up to the time of writing received a reply to my last letter. I was writing these lines to learn how you are all going on at home, trusting that this will find you all in the very best of health, as may be said of times at present. Mention I must, that Danford Fifield has written to me – he is 'Somewhere in France' in a Labour Battalion. He says that Bert Wright is somewhere out here – this I thought would not be, but perhaps it will make a man of him.

By the way dear Mother, I have written to Bob at last. I think that he was getting quite impatient with me for not writing to him. Is Lily keeping quite well now? I think it was Lily that wrote to me last saying that she would be able to send a photo of herself soon. I should like one so much.

Of course my collection all went west some considerable time ago, as I mentioned in my letter then. Where is Elsie stopping at and how is she going on?

Just tell Dad that I am coming home to spend a day or so on the river with him soon. It's to be hoped that this will come true and that every Tommy will soon be able to go home to Good old Blighty.

Well dearest Mother, I think that I have told you all this time (you know how little one can tell out here) so will now conclude with the very best of love and wishes to all. Your loving son Tom XXXXX

PS Can you send me copying ink, paper and pencils

Here is one of the letters of reply, which convey the family's feelings for Tom. It is written by Tom's mother and father and although undated, it is sent in reply to Tom's letter dated 12 September 1917.

My Dear Son

Just a few lines to you in answer to your most welcome letter. We were most delighted to think you are on the safe side still and hope that with God's will you will continue to be so. Well dear Tom, I seem to have quite a lot of news to tell you.

To begin with I must tell you Lily is rialy [really] *keeping fine and going to write to you she says.*

Your dad went fishing on Saturday but had very poor sport (nothing doing). I think that the fish are waiting for you to come back to help.

Lily has had a try but I think she must have frightened them all away She spent a day down by the river three weeks ago and got some Blackberrys and that it seems to do her a lot of good.

Elsie is still with the Muir Prices and they are very good to her. She has been with them for more than a year so Jhon [John] *is not a bad host.*

She is getting as fat as a pig I tell her and more like aunt Molly every day. You will be pleased to hear that Dorothy is going on very well at school. She is in standard six and we had a very good report of her this last term. Little Dicky is getting quite a sturdy little chap and Florrie is going on fine. I think I have told you a bit about all the family except Bob as he can speak for himself. He was up yesterday and said he had written to you last Tuesday.

'Well dear Tom the same lane has this letter. X

Sending parcel and have enclosed copy ink, pencils and just a trifle to remind you of home. Your Grandma is alright as is your brother Ben and all of us at home. Well, I will close with the best of love and good wishes from all at home. I remain your loving Mother and Dad XXXXXXXXX

(From all the kiddies)

The following is a letter from a battalion comrade who witnessed Tom's death in battle. It was received via the Army by Tom's father.

Pte. W. Elphick: 25435,
2nd Platoon,
7th Battalion KSLI
BEF
France

(Dear Mr Powis)

I am sorry about the loss of your son. He got killed by a sniper. He got to his objective and just after, he got shot in the head. Killed outright. I was not far off him. He was a good [sergeant] and new [knew] his work. You have all howers [our] sympathy from the platoon. A day after, the sniper was killed what sniped your son. It was very hot for all of us, we did well, we got a lot to be thankful for, us being alive. You have my sympathy – and your wife and family. I thought you would liked to know how your son died.

I remain
Yours sincerely
W Elphick

Another letter the family received subsequent to Tom's demise was from the battalion chaplain. It was the tradition to send this to next of kin as part of the Army's formal notification of death.

3 October
7th KSLI
BEF

Dear Mrs Powis

By now you will have received several letters telling you of the sympathy others wish to give you in your distress. A very gallant son you have lost, game right to the end, for his head lay not two feet away from a concrete 'Pill Box' in the German line. He was a magnificent solder and would have gone far had his life not been cut short. Always very smart, always very thoughtful and I always liked to think of him as a friend of mine. He is a big loss to the battalion. His career was being watched also by those outside it and they also are very grieved. We would ask you to accept our very sincere sympathy and hope that you may feel the great consolation of God in your sorrow, feeling that your son's young life has not been wasted and he is growing in strength and knowledge in the nearer presence of God.

I am yours very sincerely P. Erskine-Lee (Chaplain)

Another letter was sent by Chaplain Erskine-Lee - it is assumed to be in response to a thankyou letter he received from Mrs Powis enquiring about Tom's burial details.

25/10/17
7th KSLI
BEF

Dear Mrs Powis,

We all wish as much as you do Edith, that your little son was still with us. He was one of those outstanding men who would have gone far as a soldier. I am very sorry that I can give you no further details. I think he was buried by some Australians but of this I cannot yet be positive as I have no definite news. As soon as I do I will send you a line to tell you. That boy of yours could not have got nearer the enemy if he had tried and his example to the men will live long.

I am yours sincerely
P. Erskine-Lee.

Passchendaele Campaign 1917: The Battle of Polygon Wood

The Battle of Polygon Wood was part of the Third Battle of Ypres – better known as Passchendaele – and was fought between 26 September and 3 October 1917.

Map of Passchendaele Campaign area showing Polygon Wood

The battle took place near Ypres and was fought in the area of the Menin Road and Polygon Wood, moving north up to St Julien. The overall campaign, of which Polygon Wood was the second phase, was designed to capture the huge ridge of Messines held by the German Fourth Army. The next objective was to move on through Belgium to capture the channel ports and destroy the German submarine bases, which were being used to harass British shipping. This campaign was to inflict huge casualties on both sides and was frowned on by Marshal Foch and Lloyd George.

Haig was refused permission to proceed until they gave authorisation – and that was not given until late July. The argument against was that the whole area had been been fought over many times destroying vast areas of what were once lush woodlands. Having been levelled by artillery fire from both sides it now resembled parts of the lunar landscape. Therefore it was deemed not worth the sacrifice of the huge Allied resources needed to take it. The Americans were arriving in ever greater numbers and it was reasoned that it would be better to wait for the build up of these forces in order to facilitate a combined operation that would drive the Germans out of Flanders permanently and help end the war more quickly. Haig was to have his way and the campaign resulted in over

Tyne Cot Commonwealth War Cemetery

250,000 BEF casualties, once again for a very few miles of captured territory, all of which were retaken in the German Spring Offensive of 1918.

Local News relating to a Wellington Serviceman

The Wrekin District Roll of Honour (1988) records the following entry for Tom Powis: *17118 - Sgt. Thomas Albert Powis, 7th Battalion, KSLI. Eldest son of Mr & Mrs R. Powis of 34, Ladycroft, Wellington. Killed in action at the Battle of Polygon Wood, 26 September 1917. Enlisted in 1915 and after training at Pembroke was sent to NCO's training centre at Oswestry. Killed by shellfire* within 2 feet of German concrete pillbox. Previously worked at the CWS at Wellington, Oakengates and assistant manager at the Trench Branch. Age 20.*

---

*This report, which contrasts the earlier explanation of Sergeant Powis' death (sniper fire versus shellfire) is not a deliberate error on the part of the publication. Information about local servicemen was scarce and patchy at the time, and remains so. Family-held documents may not have been available to the compilers of the Wrekin District Roll of Honour. The other primary reason for lack of information about servicemen is that the majority of First World War records for lower ranks of non-commissioned officers, such as sergeants down to privates, were destroyed in the fire of the Army Records Centre in Arnside Street during the 1940 London Blitz in the Second World War.

Paying the Price

Wellington's Mounting Casualties as reported in *The Journal*

It was surprising in many ways that local newspapers such as *The Journal* were not banned from reporting casualty figures and printing photos of local men injured or killed.

DORA still held sway and as her grip grew ever tighter on the media, newspaper reports became more problematic. Newspapers and magazines were closed down for printing articles that were deemed to be in breach of the act.

The following two accounts were told to me by local Sue Hood about her Wellington relatives in the Great War. The first is about her great uncle, Private Albert Roberts who was with 10/KSLI:

Great Uncle Albert Roberts, who was my maternal grandmother Daisy's brother, was killed in action in 1918 in a battle along the Lys Canal in Saint Floris, aged just 21.

He was a Private with the KSLI 10th Battalion and a local author Phil Morris helped us trace his grave to Merville,

*Albert 'Bert' Roberts –
10/KSLI*

Albert Roberts Leebotwood Memorial

France, which my husband Jim and I visited in this centenary year [2014]. Known as Bert, he was born and first lived at Kinnerley near Oswestry. The family moved to Longnor near Leebotwood before the war (hence his name on the memorial at Leebotwood Church) and around the end of the war moved to Kynnersley near Wellington.

The second account from Sue Hood is about her grandfather, Private 14096 George Howard Teece of the 9th Battalion, Machine Gun Corps, Heavy Division, which was later reformed into the Tank Corps.

My paternal grandfather George Teece was a Wellington man who led a quiet life as a hospital porter at the local Wrekin Hospital in Holyhead Road. George had a cheerful, outgoing disposition and was loved by all; he was very modest about his achievements in life. We knew he had served in this terrible war yet he never spoke much at all about his experiences to anyone, not even to my father Raymond, the eldest of his six children or even his wife Nellie who was my grandmother. He lived a long and full life and, still residing in Wellington and passed away in 1977 aged eighty.

Although we were aware he was a medal-winning Great War veteran he rarely discussed the award with family members or even friends. During the centenary year [2014] we were sorting through his papers and were able to confirm some of the details of his medal award – the Croix de Guerre earned in 1918.

This is a French award for bravery and we were left puzzled as to

Private George Howard Teece – Tank Corps

the circumstances in which it could be conferred on a clearly heroic but modest British serviceman. George worked as an agricultural engineer's apprentice for the local firm of Corbett & Son before joining up in 1915.

His record shows Private G.H. Teece enlisted in the Army Service Corps as a private then later transferred to the Machine Gun Corps, Heavy Division, which was subsequently reformed into the Tank Corps in 1917. He served in the 9th Battalion and was fully trained for the position of tank driver class one. Although qualified he never had the opportunity to fill this post as anything other than a relief driver yet he served as a key crewman and gunner in several mass tank battles.

The engagement that brought the battalion award was the Battle of Moreuil Wood in July 1918, which was a French-led attack. As part of General Ludendorff's final offensive, which had begun in the spring, this battle was one of a series designed to crush the Allies quickly, before the newly-arrived Americans could gain a foothold along the Western Front and overturn any successes with their superior numbers. Paris came under imminent threat from German troops based just south of Amiens, who were dug in along the banks of the river Avre where they could launch a series of attacks along the front. It was clear that the Allies needed to remove this threat and so the job was allotted to the 3rd, 15th and 152nd French infantry divisions. During the planning stages it became apparent that tank support was vital for success, yet all their available strength was committed to the Marne sector offensive.

Impressed by previous engagements, the French requested support

from the British Tank Corps, who duly assigned the 9th Battalion. This would be one of the earliest occasions when the British fought a tank battle under French command and they were to support the 3rd French Infantry Division – known as La Grenadiere – at the centre of the attack.

After the first day of the battle on 23 July 1918, it was reported that the 3rd Division achieved all their objectives with the fewest casualties compared to the other two divisions which didn't fare as well. The French acknowledged that this was attributable to British tank support. The successful outcome of this engagement meant that the 9th Battalion was awarded France's highest award for bravery, the *Croix de Guerre avec Palme,* as a regimental decoration.

The motto of the 3rd Division was *Qui s'y frotte, s'y brule* (touch me and you burn) which was engraved on a brass badge with bursting grenade motif. The honour of wearing this was also conferred and added to the upper left arm of the jacket as part of the standard

RTC - 9th Battalion medal award - Croix De Guerre avec Palme

uniform of the 9th Battalion.

In a special field order General Bourgon, commander of the 3rd French Infantry Division records the following:

The 9th Battalion of British Tanks gave the Division the finest example of bravery, energy, of comradeship in action and of War Training carried to the highest degree of perfection. Their assistance enabled the Infantry to gain a brilliant victory, in which they themselves largely shared. La Grenadiere hereby addresses to its British comrades the touching expression of its gratitude and admiration.

George Teece's own 9th Battalion medal award for bravery explains that a further battle honour was conferred on him for the gallant and conspicuous action of rescuing an injured French officer under fire.

He was to rise to the rank of corporal, survive the war and return to Wellington where he married Nellie Jukes from Hadley (now in Telford) in 1925.

Sue Hood continues her story about her grandfather: *There was little*

14096 SUPPLEMENT TO THE LONDON GAZETTE, 29 NOVEMBER, 1918.

103735 Driver William Squire, M.M., 72nd Battery, Royal Field Artillery (Dundee).

201262 Corporal (acting Serjeant) Frederick George Stevenson, 9th Battalion, Tank Corps (Brookwood, Surrey).

64348 Driver Thomas Storey, 19th Divisional Ammunition Column, Royal Field Artillery (Hetton-le-Hole).

78439 Lance-Corporal George Swearer, 9th Battalion, Tank Corps (Ramsey, Hants).

23827 Serjeant William George Tallowin, A/110th Brigade, Royal Field Artillery (Hackney Wick, N.E.).

91266 Private George Howard Teece, 9th Battalion, Tank Corps (Wellington).

73408 Private Herbert Thackray, 25th Battalion, Machine Gun Corps (Burnley).

31563 Private (Lance-Corporal) Thomas Henry Vaughan, 6th Battalion, Royal West Kent Regiment, formerly 8th Battalion, Border Regiment (Boughton Heath).

91278 Private Frederick Walton, 9th Battalion, Tank Corps (Leamington).

8534 Corporal Jesse William Waters, C/62nd Brigade, Royal Field Artillery (Bickley, Kent).

95338 Private Benjamin Whale, 9th Battalion, Tank Corps (West Bromwich).

91260 Private George Frederick Percival Whittaker, 9th Battalion, Tank Corps (Brixton, S.W.).

56220 Serjeant Thomas Wilfred Williams, 25th Divisional Signal Company, Royal Engineers (Chester).

67477 Serjeant Peter Bissett Young, 72nd Battery, Royal Field Artillery (Edinburgh).

CORRECTIONS.

With reference to the award of the Croix de Guerre to Captain Gideon Johannes Joubert, South African Medical Corps, published in the 5th Supplement to the London Gazette of the 20th August, 1918, the letters "M.C." after his name should be amended to read "M.B."

London Gazette, 6th November, 1918.

Légion d'Honneur, Croix de Chevalier.

Page 13117.—Captain (acting Major) Arthur Herbert Tennyson, Lord Somers, Life Guards and Tank Corps, is now correctly described.

Decorations and Medals conferred by
HIS MAJESTY THE KING OF ITALY.

Military Order of Savoy.
Commander.

Lieutenant-General (temporary General) Frederick Rudolph, Earl of Cavan, K.P., K.C.B., M.V.O.

Order of St. Maurice and St. Lazarus.
Officer.

Lieutenant-Colonel (temporary Brigadier-General) Fernand Gustave Eugene Cannot, C.M.G., D.S.O., Army Service Corps.

Cavalier.

Brevet Major Leslie John Barley, D.S.O., Scottish Rifles, Special Reserve.

Lieutenant (temporary Captain) Francis Cuvelje Bedwell, M.C., West Yorkshire Regiment.

Quartermaster and Captain (temporary Major) James Betts, D.S.O., Army Gymnastic Staff.

Major Arthur Derry, D.S.O., Welsh Regiment.

Temporary Lieutenant Francis James Rennell Rodd, Royal Artillery.

Temporary Lieutenant-Colonel Henry Spencer Scott-Harden, Special List.

Order of the Crown of Italy.
Commander.

Temporary Major Archibald Alexander Gordon, C.B.E., M.V.O., Special List.

Captain (temporary Lieutenant-Colonel) Sir Maurice Pascal Alers Hankey, K.C.B. (Reserve of Officers).

Officer.

Brevet Colonel William Robertson, D.S.O., Royal Engineers.

Brevet Lieutenant-Colonel Frederick Courtney Tanner, D.S.O., Royal Scots.

Major (acting Lieutenant-Colonel) Reginald Henry Montagu Watson, Royal Garrison Artillery.

Cavalier.

Captain William John Fales, Middlesex Regiment (Territorial Force).

Temporary Captain (acting Major) Walter Parks, Royal Engineers.

Temporary Captain John Harold Peek, M.D., Royal Army Medical Corps.

Captain Peter David Thomas, Welsh Regiment (Territorial Force).

Order of St. Maurice and St. Lazarus.
Commander.

Colonel (temporary Major-General) Harry Davis Watson, C.B., C.M.G., C.I.E., M.V.O., Indian Army.

Lieutenant-Colonel (temporary Brigadier-General) Ralph Maximilian Yorke, D.S.O., Gloucestershire Yeomanry.

Officer.

Brevet Lieutenant-Colonel (temporary Lieutenant-Colonel) Wyndham Henry Deedes, D.S.O., King's Royal Rifle Corps.

Major (temporary Lieutenant-Colonel) Paul John Fearon, D.S.O., Royal West Surrey Regiment.

Lieutenant-Colonel James Hardie Galbraith, Highland Light Infantry (Territorial Force).

Captain (temporary Lieutenant-Colonel) Hoël Llewellyn, D.S.O., 3rd County of London Yeomanry.

The Order of the Crown of Italy.
Officer.

Temporary Major Alec Hutchinson Ashcroft, South Staffordshire Regiment (Service Battalion).

Brevet Major Richard Bolger Butler, M.C., 30th Lancers, Indian Army.

Captain (temporary Major) Robert Vere Buxton, West Kent Yeomanry, attached Imperial Camel Corps.

London Gazette caption mentions Private 14096 G. H Teece's personal award for bravery

Chad Valley Toys building - Wellington, present day

or no work after the war so Grandad joined the railways as a goods haulier based at Wellington station's goods yard. He delivered locally using a team of horses led by his favourite stallion called Enoch. He worked with the horses for another thirty years before joining local firm Chad Valley Toys and working there for five years.

After that, he worked at the Wrekin hospital as a porter and maintenance man.

The actual medals were in the possession of another Teece family member and my Aunt Linda (his daughter) and I asked for them to be returned and we had them restored and specially mounted. We loved George and Bert dearly and are grateful for their sacrifice.

Review of the Allied Army Chiefs' Prowess Regarding the War's Conduct

It is certainly true that Lloyd George was critical of the BEF Commander in Chief (C-in-C) Douglas Haig and as the war progressed and the casualties mounted, he became less and less enamoured of his lack of strategic prowess and ability to achieve a successful outcome.

British War Medal	Victory Medal	Croix de Guerre Medal

Forces War Record:-

First Name:	George Howard
Surname:	Teece
Resided Town:	Wellington
Rank:	Private
Service Number:	91266
Gallantry Awards:	Croix de Guerre
Gazette Info:	Gazette Issue 31039. Croix de Guerre. The non-commissioned officer was awarded the French decoration Croix de Guerre for distinguished services rendered during the course of the campaign.
Gazette Date:	26/11/1918 (Main Issue)
Gazette Page:	14096
Service:	British Army
Regiment:	Royal Tank Corps
Battalion:	9th Battalion

G.H. Teece's medals

He therefore placed Haig and his command under Marshal Foch who was appointed by the French Prime Minister Georges Clemenceau in 1918 as Allied Forces Commander (Allied *Généralissime*) of the Western Front.

A brilliant tactician and able leader, it could be argued that Foch presided over the most successful Allied campaigns ever fought, during the latter half of 1918.

The BEF Infantry had become an experienced battle-hardened fighting force that was well-manned, trained, equipped and highly proficient in executing tactics both as

Marshal Ferdinand Foch

part of an Allied engagement or independently in its own right. Following the disasters of the Somme and Passchendaele campaigns, the learning curve had been steep but the lessons, although expensive in terms of manpower and equipment, were well-practised and applied. Under Haig's leadership the BEF was to redeem itself and by 1918 had turned into a cohesive fighting force.

Field Marshal Sir Douglas Haig, Commander in Chief, British Army: a Brief Outline

The overall architect of the Somme and Passchendaele campaigns came of Scottish ancestry, yet despite being heir to the eponymous Scotch whisky distillery fortune, Field Marshal Sir Douglas Haig was first and foremost a career soldier.

Appointed commander in chief of the BEF on 15 November 1915, he was regarded by Winston Churchill as a skilled tactician and fine soldier, and by others as a total incompetent.

His critics portrayed him as a commanding officer who presided over an erratic, idiosyncratic and ultimately weak staff corps of officers.

There was no love lost between Haig and Lloyd George, the Prime Minister in office from 1916. He presided over a coalition cabinet riven by divided loyalties to Haig as a successful career soldier along with a vague sense of guilt at the recent dismissal and speedy ousting of his predecessor, Sir John French in 1915.

Haig is rumoured to have provided a derogatory testament concerning French's abilities to command. This brings into question where his loyalties lay, as he was his second in command, and his evidence may have influenced their decision.

Nevertheless this outcome

Sir Douglas Haig

catapulted Haig's career into the limelight, from relative obscurity to centre stage of the conflict.

Following the Passchendaele debacle, Lloyd George demanded that Haig serve under the recently appointed C-in-C of the Allied Forces, Field Marshal Ferdinand Foch.

It is not mentioned in detail whether they enjoyed each other's company but Haig did stubbornly command the BEF in isolation. Based in his own headquarters, he only answered direct summonses to attend Allied staff officer meetings called by Foch.

In the end Haig only survived as BEF C-in-C because eventually the successes began to outweigh the failures. Under Haig, the BEF became more battle-hardened and improved diligently following the disastrous first Somme campaign. Within 16 months they were able to achieve some of the most spectacular military successes ever seen on the Western Front.

Although considered to be lacking intellectually, Haig's time at Brasenose College, Oxford University (1880- 83) and a further two years at Staff College in Camberley, Surrey (1896-97) would seem to cast doubt on this assumption. Haig was first and foremost a cavalryman and a veteran of several colonial wars. Prompted by his chief of intelligence, John Charteris, he was erroneously and steadfastly convinced that the Germans were on the verge of collapse when he proposed the Somme campaign.

The Big Push – the first of many termed as such – was planned in response to the shattering losses suffered by the French at Verdun in early 1916.

Haig's relentless notions persisted even after the Somme campaign and were based on the false contention that the German military machine was close to collapse and only required a single decisive hammer blow to be delivered by the BEF.

Haig could then send in his first love, the cavalry, to mop up any resistance and thereby consolidate the positions gained. He persisted in thinking that a war of attrition was justified and therefore right to pursue, despite the heavy reciprocal losses suffered by the BEF. When engaging the *Bosch* (the German Army), which consisted of modern, seasoned, well-equipped frontline infantrymen, who on balance were winning the war, he continually underestimated their capabilities.

Somehow the Germans always managed to survive and endure despite everything Haig's Army threw at them and continued to harass the Allied advance.

His supervision of subordinates was debatable as he never seemed to question or critique their effectiveness, particularly in the case of his second-in-command, General Sir Henry Rawlinson.

General H. Rawlinson

Rawlinson's battle plans and strategies were never scrutinised for their feasibility or potential material gain to the BEF or Allied cause in general. His man-management style, by contrast, was coloured by his bombastic approach and invariably he pushed through his own version of plans, resenting interference or criticism from any quarter. Haig's leadership was considerably weakened by this state of affairs and brought into question his overall effectiveness and achievements as commander.

Whether this was down to officer etiquette or simple lack of command skills, we will never know as Haig skips over that part in his official published memoirs, gleaned from contemporary hand-written war diaries, later rewritten with the help of his wife.

We do find that command structure and staff management interrelationship courses were curiously absent from the curriculum of most officer training academies during the First World War although some staff officer training recommenced later in the war.

The tragedy for Haig was his Victorian perception of what was required by an officer in command. Qualities such as a sense of loyalty to one's men and a duty to the flag, corps and honour of the battlefield were admirable but did nothing to prepare the modern officer to command vast armies fighting a multi-level, multi-weaponed modern war. Once in command, their decisions in single engagements or lengthy campaigns could result in a casualty rate of thousands or even tens of thousands.

Judged in the cold light of history, Haig presided over the biggest losses ever suffered by the British Army in a single day and in a single engagement, as well as the greatest successes in the latter stages of the war on the Western Front.

When the appalling casualty figures came through from the adjutant general's office for the first day of the Somme, Haig famously recorded in his field diary:

2nd July – 1916 –

The AG [adjutant general] reported today that the total casualties are estimated at over 40,000 to date. This cannot be considered severe in view of the numbers engaged and the length of front attacked... .

Such apparent callousness was uncharacteristic of Haig, who was a deeply religious Anglican, loved and respected by his men throughout the war. Indeed he was so moved by the plight of the veterans after the war that he set up the Haig Fund. This was subsequently taken over by the British Legion who adopted the Flanders poppy as the emblem for their annual appeal and retained his name for the fund, which is still used to this day.

Although universally condemned for his flawed military strategies, he was a leader of men whose military foresight convinced him that the war would last longer than first thought and that the aeroplane had great potential as a weapon of modern warfare.

At his death in 1928 he was eulogised. Yet within ten years he would be vilified in the press as a butcher for the profligate numbers of men lost in the wasteful battles of the Great War.

The Last German Offensive: Spring Campaign 1918
Ludendorff's Final Gamble

General Erich Ludendorff's *Kaiserschlacht* (Kaiser's Battle) campaign called Operation *Michael* was one of four and was launched

in March 1918. The other three campaigns, *Georgette*, *Gneisenau* and *Blücher-Yorck* were designed as feints to draw out the Allied Forces and bolster the main attack in the lightly-defended area of the Somme.

It was the last big opportunity to crush a defeated France – whose armies had begun to mutiny due to poor equipment and lack of supplies including

General Erich Ludendorff,
Second in Command,
German Army

rations – and a weakened BEF reeling from the expensive Nivelle and Passchendaele campaigns. On the Eastern front, opposition had all but collapsed, due to the cessation of fighting by the Russians after the Communist revolution of October 1917, thereby ending a major ally's support. The Russians new *Bolshevik* government, signed the Treaty of Brest-Litovsk with Germany on 3 March 1918, which freed 50 German infantry divisions for redeployment on the Western Front.

With everything to gain and the war looking lost for the Allies, Ludendorff's priority was to drive a wedge between the English and French forces whilst pushing towards the channel ports. It was crucial to achieve all this before the Americans arrived in sufficient numbers to turn the tables in equipment and manpower.

At 4:40 am on 21 March, the German artillery opened up for five hours followed by waves of stormtroopers who overran positions on the Somme which were, as they suspected, lightly

Paul von Hindenburg – CIC of German Army

defended. All went well at first, with the recapture of Passchendaele. This new front broadened out to push the Allies back. It was becoming a more mobile war, less trenchbound and the tide seemed to be turning in their favour.

This prompted Haig to issue his famous 'backs to the wall' order of 11 April which said: 'The enemy appears to have the advantage and we must fight with our backs to the wall.' Inevitably the German momentum faltered due to lack of supplies and Ludendorff's chronic inability to consolidate the gains made before moving on to the next objective.

The German advance finally ground to a halt at the battle of Amiens. Ludendorff was to record in his diary that this was the 'blackest day of the German Army'. Amid a welter of claim and counterclaim by Ludendorff and the general staff who argued continually amongst themselves, German resistance collapsed. Ludendorff would blame his men, his staff and the government for the 'stab in the back' conspiracy that the armistice and the treaty represented until long after the war ended.

Although effectively the chief of the German land forces, he was technically number two to Paul von Hindenburg C-in-C of the Army who in turn reported to the Kaiser.

The Allies' Final Push: the Closing Great Battles

Under the brilliant Marshal Foch not only did the Allies regain ground, they fought some of the greatest set piece battles of the war as the Germans retreated across France and Belgium. The Allied armies now launched a Grand Offensive across the whole front. The Franco-American attack on 26 September in the Meuse-Argonne area was quickly followed the following day by the British First and Third armies attacking towards Cambrai. On the 28th the French, Belgian and British forces pushed on towards Ypres and the final stage of the offensive on the 29th was conducted by the British Fourth and French First armies.

The Germans ended up fighting from behind their own Hindenburg Line. Much like the French version (the Maginot Line) this comprised a vast network of defensive fortifications extending along its own Belgian border. Although heavy fighting lay ahead, the final assault came as the Allies broke through an immensely strong belt of defences including a portion of the St. Quentin Canal. As the Allies overcame successive defence lines, undermining morale and unit cohesion, substantial numbers of German troops surrendered or deserted and on 26 October Ludendorff was dismissed.

Sixteen days later a group of German generals crossed the line and signed an armistice.

The American Expeditionary Forces (AEF) under C-in-C General John J. Pershing were to impact finally on the Germans' fighting capacity if only thanks to their strength of numbers.

Altogether the USA enlisted one-and-a-half million men for overseas duty and saw 50,385 killed in action, 54,754 dead from disease and 260,000 wounded or disabled. Pershing's autocratic leadership style meant that he refused to place his

General John. J.
Pershing, C-in-C AEF

men under the control of Marshal Foch. Although always cooperating and coordinating with Allied campaigns he consistently managed and directed the AEF's fighting separately.

The Raid on Zeebrugge

In a previous war news report in the edition dated 5 December 1914 *The Journal* ran the following item about the Belgian port of Zeebrugge from a correspondent based in Amsterdam:

During the last few days, the harbour buildings and works at Zeebrugge, which had suffered severely by the British Bombardment, had been repaired. The material for the construction of the German Submarines brought to Zeebrugge, was much greater than was first supposed and that attacks on French and British vessels might be expected soon. Zeebrugge would in fact, become the greatest German naval base for Submarines.

These words proved to be prophetic and by the end of 1917, the German submarine blockade operating out of Zeebrugge was causing severe shortages to the Allies.

Sir John Jellicoe proposed a raid on the submarine base to neutralise the menace. He argued that it was vital to block the exits from the port and this could be achieved by using old hulks packed with concrete and sinking them as blockships at the entrance to the Bruges Canal. The next phase was to land Royal Marines via the cruiser HMS *Vindictive* on the mile-long Zeebrugge mole to destroy the formidable shore batteries. The actual operation began on 23 April 1918, under the command of Admiral Sir Roger Keyes. Due to bad weather and worse luck the covering smoke screen was blown away to reveal the raiding force. HMS *Vindictive* took so heavy a pounding from the coastal defences she could not land her marines, who suffered heavy casualties.

The shore batteries disabled other blockships and prevented total blockage by the remainder of the ships, thus allowing only partial access via the port's canal.

Both sides claimed victory and the British awarded eight Victoria Crosses. However the Germans had cleared the blockage completely within a few days and were back to normal operations. Although less than successful the operation, having been preceded by RAF bombing raids, was regarded as the first tri-service maritime assault of modern times.

Aftermath

How News of the Armistice Was Reported in Wellington

When the hostilities ceased, *The Journal*, in common with all British newspapers, brandished delighted decisive Headlines. *The War is Over* it screamed to its Wellington readership, which had

The Journal - *War is Over - front page November 1918*

Wellington Market Hall celebration –Children's Armistice Tea Party

WAR ENDED.
ARMISTICE SIGNED
AND
FIGHTING OVER.

The war has ended. This great news as conveyed to the people this morning these words : –

The Prime Minister makes the following announcement :

The armistice was signed at 5 a.m this morning, and hostilities are to cease on all fronts at 11 a.m. to-day been holding its breath for over four long years. Only now was it able to release a collective sigh of relief. Relief to have survived the combat, to be able to start life anew, and to know their loved ones were finally safe from harm.

Joy at the war's end was illustrated by a simple celebration held in Wellington. Inside the market hall, management cleared the floor and put up trestle tables to treat the local children to a special armistice tea party.

Post War Changes: Remorse and Mourning Nationally and in Wellington

With the dust settled over the battlefields and the guns remaining silent, a time of contemplation descended over the land. Britain remembered its war dead and considered the cost in terms of lives lost and financial hardships incurred.

People began to challenge openly the reasons for the fighting and its legitimacy by posing the ultimate question: what had it all been for? The 'land fit for heroes' that had been promised to Britain's fighting men on their return from war had failed to materialise.

In fact, they came back to an atmosphere of chronic sickness. It was speculated that the Spanish flu pandemic of 1919 to 1921, which wiped out fifty million people worldwide, could have originated from soldiers returning home after contracting trench fever, which then mutated.

All of this conjecture was undermining the mood of patriotism that had launched the war and sustained the British people through the dark days of mounting casualties.

The architect Sir Edwin Lutyens was tasked to design a temporary war memorial for Whitehall in London to act as a focus for local and national mourning at the Peace Day Parade on 11 November 1919. His design comprised a single huge block, decorated with flags and laurel wreaths. Called the Cenotaph (meaning literally 'empty tomb') it commemorates all the war dead. It was not conceived as a permanent fixture, constructed originally in wood and plaster to simulate stone. However, it proved such a success at the first commemoration service that it was replaced for the next ceremony with the permanent stone structure we see today. The practice of commemoration every

Cenotaph, Whitehall, London

Armistice Day was to prove so popular with the country that it became an annual event.

In November 1920, the national outpouring of grief culminated in the ceremony of the unknown warrior buried in Westminster Abbey. This involved the random selection of one of the unidentified bodies recovered from the Western Front to be given a state funeral as a national salute to the fallen. It helped console the thousands of mourners unable to locate their missing servicemen, who were comforted by the notion that it was possibly their own dead relative laid to rest in the tomb.

Wellington had paid a heavy price in terms of its war dead as 182

Lych Gate Memorial, Church Green, Wellington containing Brass plaques

Brass plaques - Lych Gate Memorial

serving men and women were never to return from the conflict. Each of their names grace the brass plaques of the Lych Gate Memorial at All Saints Church, which was opened to the public in 1922.

Britain's steadfast Dunkirk spirit, so evident in the Second World War, was born out of the Great War's shared adversities. The whole country had to endure large scale losses of both civilian and military manpower. No one will deny that the Second World War was fought for clear cut motives such as international survival against a dreadful fascist tyranny. Yet the motivation behind the Great War's conflict is much more complex. It comprises many facets of differing national self-interests such as colonial rivalry and territorial disputes.

Similar to Hitler's Germany, most combatants accepted that such devastating manpower losses were inevitable if they were to achieve their goal. However, by the end of the Great War, this universal acceptance of war as a noble and natural part of human affairs was discredited.

The first and fundamental post-war change was the end of government by dynastic rule, which led to greater democratic freedoms for most European countries. Before the war, the dynastic system reigned supreme across the major western powers of Europe.

Aftershocks: How the Political Map Changed in Europe Post 1918

As a shattered Germany adjusted to peace, its people rejected Kaiser Wilhelm, and the *Hohenzollern* dynasty blaming both for their predicament. Overhelmed by the financial meltdown it dabbled with republicanism and established the Weimar Republic. The resulting social and political chaos persisted throughout the 1920s. The effects of crippling war reparations, leading to hyperinflation and the collapse of the currency, were to pave the way for general unrest.

When Germany defaulted on its payments in 1919, the Allies annexed the border and created a demilitarized zone called the Rhineland. This was seen as a compromise to appease the French who had argued for complete dismemberment of the country after having stripped its armed forces. This was to fuel the rise and spread of diverse political ideologies in Germany including communism and ultimately fascism, masquerading as socialism.

One such faction was the fledgling National Socialist Party, latterly contracted to 'Nazi' and led by an ex-corporal in the Kaiser's First World War Army – a certain Adolf Hitler.

In Italy fundamental change came with the inception of the National Fascist Party, formed in 1921 by an ex-lawyer called Benito Mussolini. Known as *Il Duce* (the leader) by his black-shirted followers, Mussolini's party sought power in 1922. Its epic march on Rome resulted in a landslide victory and the collapse of the existing government, which abdicated in favour of a fascist-style alliance which ruled constitutionally for several years. In 1925, abandoning all democratic pretence, *Il Duce* replaced this with his own branded version of fascism. He tightened his political stranglehold and yet another shattered European regime fell under the influence of a power-hungry dictator.

Belgium's armies were put under King Albert I's command and they held the low-lying areas between Ypres and Nieuwpoort on the coast but did not participate in any major allied engagements until the final month of the war. Belgium had suffered the nightmare scenario of battles fought on its soil from the first day to the last and paid a heavy price with fatalities numbering over 40,000 with more than 100,000 injured.

In Russia the legacy of war overturned 300 years of Romanoff dynastic rule. With the deposing of the Tsar in 1917 and the establishment of the world's first workers republic (or *soviet*), the country changed its name to the Union of Soviet Socialist Republics (USSR). Thus the first communist regime was born with all its attendant Cold War fallout that divided Europe well into the modern era. Its final collapse wouldn't be until 1991 when it became the Russian Federation.

The Great War was termed 'the war to end all wars' yet we know this was patently not the case. Even after this amount of time, with all the horrors this war and others have produced, it is still manifestly clear that man's appetite for war remains undiminished. In fact the world has experienced continuous conflict, in one place or another, since the signing of the armistice document inside a railway carriage in the

Forest of Compiegne in 1918. The Cold War era is within living memory and few can forget the sense of doom as the Cuban Missile Crisis unfolded during the early 1960s threatening global atomic warfare.

Many of those involved in the Great War were convinced mankind had been poised on the brink of self-destruction. Some combat survivors were never to recover emotionally or financially. Others gave more than was expected and were to lose the future lifeblood of their families. Not since the Black Death of the fourteenth century had Britain and Europe suffered such a sudden reduction in its seed population. It wasn't just members of the Armed Forces who were lost but also civilian men, women and children. Killed by air raids, naval gunfire and the sundry effects of war, they totalled some 4.5 million Europe-wide.

Casualty figures for the armed services on all sides were staggering with approximately 31 million dead, wounded or missing. Vast numbers of injured servicemen also suffered permanent physical and mental disability as a direct result of the conflict. For the first time in human history mechanised slaughter on the battlefield was applied on an unparalleled scale. It was destined to be a war of firsts, on the pathway to militaristic wholesale destruction. It also paved the way for the development of weapons of mass destruction.

Every mode and method of mechanical device conjured by man's limitless ingenuity was brought into play whether in the air, at sea, or on land. Sometimes in concert with other weapons or tactics, sometimes simultaneously, but always with the same devastating result. It ranged from chemical weapons, with all their deadly gas variants deployed on a mass but haphazard scale, to powered flight raining death from the skies with aerial bombardment by the Zeppelin airships in direct contravention of a pact signed in 1899. These monster dirigibles (flying gas-bags) caused 3,000 civilian casualties in UK mainland bombing raids. We are familiar with the Luftwaffe's sustained blitz in the Second World War, but these shocking air-raid statistics, another first for the First World War, seem to have slipped under history's radar. The tank, aeroplane and submarine were relatively new inventions that were used mostly later in the war, with only varying success. The commander of the 500 tonne submarine UB-68,

Oberleutnant Karl Doenitz, was part of the first German submarine fleet to develop the techniques required to effectively blockade Allied shipping in the Atlantic.

Losses of British merchant shipping exceeded that of the Americans who were prompted to join the Great war as a direct result of their own shipping losses to this blockade.

Nearly eight million tonnes of marine trade were lost thanks to the German policy of indiscriminate attacks. A key event was the sinking of the British Cunard liner RMS *Lusitania* by the U-boat U-20 on 7 May 1915 with the loss of 1,198 passengers and crew including 128 neutral Americans. She was rumoured to be carrying munitions (confirmed recently by underwater marine archeology) which made her a legitimate target for the German submarine fleet. One of the main reasons

Admiral Karl Doenitz, circa 1943

US President Woodrow Wilson decided to join the Allies in 1917, was to end this seaborne menace by helping to defeat Germany. This tactical experience enabled Doenitz, who became Admiral of the Fleet in 1940, to formulate his 'wolfpack' strategy. During the Second World War, this was applied with such devastating and ruthless effect in the same ocean for the same reasons – the sinking of Allied shipping. The 'U-boat scourge', as it was termed in the later war, was the single threat that (as he admitted afterwards) terrified Winston Churchill the most.

The real Great War stories are the ones involving the ordinary citizens of a once great Imperial nation that we have endeavoured to tell in this book. Some historians maintain that the Allied cause was futile. Its reasons for prosecuting the war were imbecilic when compared to the credible and necessary objectives of the Allies in the Second World War, determined to defeat and eradicate despotism and fascism.

The physical effects of conflict across Europe during the the First World War were relatively minor when contrasted with the scale of devastation suffered in the Second World War.

Thus the physical scars left on the UK by the Great War were erased quickly and slipped from the public consciousness. This is more a tribute to the stoicism and stiff upper lip of the British character than the realisation of the lasting impact the conflict left nationally and in Wellington.

It would be several years before the effects of war permeated the fabric of a British society stuck fast in the nineteenth century with its imperial outlook and rigid class structure. Fortunately, it involved relatively little rebuilding of the UK's towns and cities, unlike the scale required after the Second World War. With the physical scars healed the cultural and psychological impact was to pervade much deeper into the nation's psyche. For the first time in history the powers that be had to face a backlash from the millions of ordinary people whose relatives had paid the price of victory in blood across the Allied nations and particularly in Britain. Sons, brothers, uncles and fathers were eradicated wholesale from a generation by simply answering the call to defend King and country. Their relatives' grief fomented into deep-seated resentment and heartfelt betrayal that led to a great distrust of politicians and figures of authority in general. Although statistically only 1.6 per cent of the population (forces and civilian) in the UK, comprising 12 per cent of the service personnel, were killed and 44 per cent wounded, it was still a major catastrophe that was to scar the minds and hearts of people for generations. This was evidenced in the growing social strife in Britain that resulted in the rise of union power and socialist politics culminating in the general strike of 1926. This reaction was viewed in some quarters as a clarion call to arms using the model of the Russian revolution, which saw the people rise against their capitalist masters.

The British nation had to face up to the economic loss wrought by the rigours of conducting total warfare and the cost was somewhere in excess of £13 billion.

To offset this, the UK borrowed from the Americans and coined the term 'the national debt'. The immeasurable impact of the war, both culturally and economically, changed the social map of Britain forever.

It was the beginning of the end of the rigid class structure that had dominated the country, and facilitated the path for the ordinary masses to rise. Prior to the war, towns across the country were largely self-governing and self-reliant for food and general supplies. At the time there were no motorways to transport bulk items, only canals or railways and basic two-lane roads.

Not long into the twentieth century, railways were interacting between towns, cities and ports and during the Great War, they would be used to transport over one million men as well as massive amounts of machinery to the battle front.

France and Germany had laid contingency plans to defend their territories using railways as far back as 1833. However the range of means we have to transport foodstuffs and commodities today was not available then.

Prior to the Great War, each town, including Wellington, was self-sufficient and therefore autonomous. Its life and development was determined by size and geographic location and not dependent on the railway network. Horsepower and limited lorry power (which was increasingly popular after the war) handled local distribution. There were no building programmes supported by large independent construction companies bidding for housing contracts. The most comprehensive social housing complexes were commissioned by individual companies such as Cadbury's Bournville and the Sunlight soap owners ostensibly to house their respective workforces and hailed in their time as models of benevolence. There were no chainstores or supermarkets to keep the nation supplied with all manner of fresh foods and goods. Each town fed, clothed and housed their most underprivileged citizens themselves, thus handling their lives from the cradle to the grave. This feudal outlook helped assert the rigid class system, which kept the lower classes in their place economically and politically, and retarded the development of an upwardly mobile working class.

Clearly the greatest effect of the war upon society was the wholesale change of structure from within. Women had left their traditional domestic roles behind and joined the manufacturing industries. Their increase in earning power meant that household incomes improved, resulting in better diets and greater social freedom for women. These were mostly reneged upon after the war's end, inflicted by a global depression and trade unions forcing businesses to give jobs back to returning male war veterans.

However, as the vital role women played during the war became more widely recognised, it benefited the causes of women's suffrage. Lloyd George and other cabinet members promised to meet their demands after the war's end.

This culminated in the statutory inauguration of women's voting rights brought in by an act of parliament in 1918. Although restricted to married women over thirty, it was later fully instituted to include all women over 21 in 1928.

The Great War required a vast amount of resource materials, other than manpower, and organising this was a nightmare. The logistics of moving food, basic supplies, munitions, transport, stationery materials not to mention troops, weapons and support equipment, such as horses, on a vast scale were completely new and mind boggling for those involved. It is difficult for younger generations, born into today's fast-paced world, to understand just how bereft of communication technology, society was then. Everyday life ran at a slower pace by comparison, One wonders how people managed to get on with life when mass slaughter was taking place. The media did its best to dilute

The Journal: *printed casualty lists for the war*

the facts. Very early on in the war, casualty figures were distorted or hidden from the general public, resulting in a misleading perception of the war's progress. No statistics were kept on the impact this huge loss of life had on generations of families, communities and local economies in Britain or abroad. Newspapers were the only media outlets and it is difficult to describe adequately their power and influence on the readership they served.

'The People's War' as it was described, meant that for the first time in mass conflict the ordinary working class man fought and died side by side with the aristocrat.

Only the circumstances of death made them equal.

At the end of the war, a grassroots cynicism developed organically and this helped establish the great humanitarian institutions we recognise today, such as charity foundations and anti-war movements.

Armistice and the Signing of the Treaty of Versailles

After the signing of the armistice on 11 November 1918, the Allies believed Germany should be held to account for the expense caused by the physical damage to Europe's countries, particularly Belgium and France.

This was unprecedented. No other conflict had resulted in such action being taken against the losers. Having sued for peace, the Germans and Austro-Hungarians had assumed that everyone would

Palace of Versailles

Hall of Mirrors - Palace of Versailles - Allied nations gather for Peace Treaty in 1919

shake hands and move back to a position of co-operation whilst rebuilding took place. They were to be sadly mistaken and deeply humiliated.

On 28 June 1919 in the Hall of Mirrors at the Palace of Versailles in France, once the playground of the French Sun King Louis XIV, Germany and Austria were made to sign a peace treaty document. Not only did it detail territory surrender but also swingeing reparations of £6,600 billion: this being the total cost of the war as agreed by all the European Allies and the USA.

These terms would not only destroy both empires, but they would bankrupt their nations.

The Austro-Hungarian empire was abolished and the new countries of Poland, Hungary and Czechoslovakia emerged along with the freed Serbian and Slavic nations of Albania, Bulgaria and Yugoslavia.

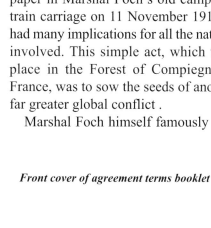

American version of cartoon of Reparations (equivalent amount shown in dollars) as per terms of the Treaty of Versailles

When the war ended, with the signing of a piece of paper in Marshal Foch's old campaign train carriage on 11 November 1918, it had many implications for all the nations involved. This simple act, which took place in the Forest of Compiegne in France, was to sow the seeds of another far greater global conflict .

Marshal Foch himself famously said

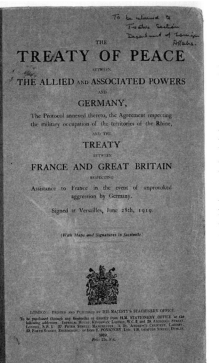

Front cover of agreement terms booklet

Order of service booklet Lych Gate dedication ceremony, 1922

after the Peace treaty signing: *'This is no surrender, merely a temporary truce for twenty years.'* His prophetic words were to come true when in 1939 the Second World War commenced. Adolf Hitler was to take his revenge and expunge the humiliation visited on Germany by forcing the French to sign their surrender document at exactly the same location, in Compiegne, after their capitulation in 1940.

With typical Nazi efficiency the site was then destroyed, including Foch's carriage.

(The museum exhibit we see today is a replica – lovingly restored to its former glory.)

Wellington's Great War Memorials

No words can describe the devastating and lasting effects war had on the ordinary people, nationally and in Wellington. Such was the outcry, people from across the land raised the funds to erect various monuments to the fallen.

Building began enthusiastically as sculptors, architects and builders erected hundreds of them nationwide. Some were not of the highest artistic quality but were definitely the result of a heartfelt expression of sentiment from communities who had sent their loved ones to war.

Wellington's centrepiece memorial is Lych Gate at All Saints Church, which was erected and inaugurated in a civic ceremony in 1922. The name 'lych' (Anglo Saxon for corpse) was suggested as a nod to ancient times when ordinary people delivered their dead to the church gate. This ritual was viewed as the secular world handing loved ones over to the care of the spiritual world for Christian burial.

Unfortunately this simple civic ceremony designed to commemorate Wellington's war heroes would be overshadowed by a scandal.

The Lych Gate Memorial Scandal

The brass memorial plaques decorated with the list of Wellington's war dead, were unveiled on 6 May 1922 when the lych gate was presented to the Urban District Council by the Independent Conservative MP Major General Sir Charles Vere Ferrers Townshend KCB, DSO.

He was elected in 1919 on a tide of populism and like many people at the time, traded on his war service to achieve public office. He duly

Roll of Honour.

The following is a list of Officers and Other Ranks of the various branches of His Majesty's Forces from Wellington Urban District who fell in the Great War, and whose names are inscribed on the Memorial Tablets in the Lychgateway.

Adams, G.	Private	K.S.L.I.
Adderley, F.	Private	K.S.L.I.
Arnold, E. W.	Private	Hereford Regt.
Birch, Laura M.		W.R.A.F.
Bailey, J. T.	Private	K.S.L.I.
Baker, W.	Sergt.	K.S.L.I.
Baxter, F.	Private	R.W.F.
Beard, C. J.	Driver	R.A.S.C.
Beddoe, W. J.	L.T.O.	H.M.S. Pincher
Beech, W.	Private	K.S.L.I.
Bennett, W. C.	Driver	R.E.
Bloomer, R. C.	Private	K.S.L.I.
Bowen, C. W.	L/Cpl.	K.S.L.I.
Bradley, L. J.	Private	R.W.F.
Bradley, J. R.	Private	R.W.F.
Bradley, J. T.	Private	K.S.L.I.
Brisbourne, G. O. L.	Private	Border Regt.
Brittain, R. A. H.	2nd Lieut.	R.A.F.
Cadman, M. D.	Surgeon-Prob.	H.M.S. Rival
Carver, W. T.	Sergt.	Liverpool Regt.
Cartwright, J.	Private	S.W.B.
Charles, H.	Private	K.S.L.I.
Challoner, A.	Private	K.S.L.I.
Chilton, H.	2nd Lieut.	Lancas. Fus.
Churm, H.	Private	Suffolks
Clarke, E.	Private	Monmouths
Cotton, R.	Private	K.S.L.I.
Cotton, J.	Private	K.S.L.I.
Cruise, W. H.	Private	K.S.L.I.
Cureton, W.	Private	K.S.L.I.
Davies, L.	Bombdr.	R.F.A. (N.Z.)
Davies, W.	Private	S.W.B.
Davies, G.	Private	K.S.L.I.
Davies, A.	Private	Somerset L. I.
Dodson, C.	Sergt.	M.G.C.
Doody, A.	Private	Grenadier Guards
Duckett, J. O.	Private	K.S.L.I.
Dunn, A.	Cpl.	K.S.L.I.
Edwards, H. G.	Bomdr.	R.F.A.
Elcocks, R.	Private	R.W.F.
Elson, W. A.	Private	S.W.B.

List of the fallen (182 names) of Wellington war dead (as shown in the original Order of Service Booklet)

Elson, C. S.	P.O.	H.M.S. Impregnable
Elphick, J. F.	Private	K.S.L.I.
Emery, C. T.	Private	K.S.L.I.
Emery, H.	Private	K.S.L.I.
Espley, H.	Private	New Zealand E. F.
Evans, R. W.	Sergt.	Cheshires
Evans, J.	L/Cpl.	S.I.Y.
Evans, J.	Sergt.	R.H.A.
Fleming, H. J.	Private	K.S.L.I.
Fletcher, T.	Private	K.S.L.I.
Fletcher, J.	Private	K.S.L.I.
Fletcher, C.	2nd Lieut.	R.A.F.
Foulkes, H.	Private	K.S.L.I.
Fox, G. J.	L/Cpl.	K.S.L.I.
Fox, C. T.	Gunner	R.F.A.
Fox, A. W.	Private	K.S.L.I.
Fox, G.	Gunner	R.G.A.
Francis, E. R.	Private	R.W.F.
Frost, G. F.	Air Mec.	R.N.A.S.
Green, W. J.	Private	K.S.L.I.
Greenfield, G. R.	Corpl.	K.S.L.I.
Griffiths, A. R.	L/Cpl.	Gordon Hdrs.
Griffiths, E. V.	Pioneer	R.E.
Griffiths, H.	Private	Scots Guards
Griffiths, J.	Private	M.G.C.
Gough, J. C.	Corpl.	York & Lancs. Regt.
Gough, A. S.	Private	R.M.L.I.
Gwynne, H.	Private	K.S.L.I.
Harris, S.	Private	K.S.L.I.
Hall, S.	Private	Sherwood Foresters
Harvey, W. M.	Lieut.	K.S.L.I.
Haynes, A. J.	Farrier-Sergt.	R.F.A.
Harper, J. F.	Bomdr.	R.F.A.
Harris, J. H.	Private	K.S.L.I.
Healey, F. J.	Private	K.S.L.I.
Healey, G.	Private	Northumberland Fus.
Healey, J.	Corpl.	K.S.L.I.
Henn, E. G.	Private	Welsh Regt.
Hodgson, A. E. S.	2nd Lieut.	Yorks. & Lancs. Regt.
Holloway, S.	L/Cpl.	K.S.L.I.
Horton, W. P.	L/Cpl.	London Regt.
Horton, J. N.	L/Cpl.	London Regt.
Hotchkiss, C. R.	Private	M.G.C.
Humphries, W. E.	L/Cpl.	K.S.L.I.
Jarvis, J. T.	L/Cpl.	K.S.L.I.
Jarvis, J. M.	L/Cpl.	K.S.L.I.
Jarvis, J. H.	Private	R.N.V.R.
Jauncey, J.	Private	R. Warwicks
Jones, J. H.	Private	K.S.L.I.
Jones, J. S.	Ldg. Stoker	R.N.V.R.
Jones, B.	L/Cpl.	Cheshires
Jones, R. W.	Corpl.	R.E.
Jones, H. W.	Private	Welsh Regt.
Jones, S. W.	Private	K.S.L.I.
Jones, N.	Private	R. Berks.
Johnson, H.	Private	K.S.L.I.

Kirkham, T. J.	Private	R.A.V.C.
Langley, W.	C.S.M.	R.D.C.
Leigh, S.	Private	Cheshires
Lloyd, J. W.	Private	Cheshires
Lloyd, G.	Gunner	R.G.A.
Lloyd, H. C.	Corpl.	Somerset L. I.
Lloyd, S. J.	Gunner	R.F.A.
Lowndes, S.	Private	K.S.L.I.
Lucas, C.	Private	K.S.L.I.
Lyon, C. E.	2nd Lieut.	R.F.A.
Magness, A. G.	Sergt.	R.W.F.
Magness, F.	L/Cpl.	R.E.
Mansfield, G. H.	Private	Bedfords
Mason, F. W.	Air-Mec.	R.A.F.
Moore, J.	L/Cpl.	K.S.L.I.
Morgan, R. C.	Private	R. Fus.
Morris, A. A.	L/Cpl.	K.S.L.I.
Morris, R. H.	2nd Lieut.	R. Warwicks
Mumford, H.	Rifleman	Ontago Hussars
Naggington, F.	Private	K.S.L.I.
Newnes, W.	Private	Herefords
Nicholls, J.	Private	K.S.L.I.
Norris, W. A.	Private	K.S.L.I.
Paddock, H. L.	Major	Sherwood Foresters
Padmore, F.	Private	Innis. Fus.
Paget, J. W.	Private	K.S.L.I.
Palmer, W. H.	Private	K.S.L.I.
Pankhurst, A. W.	Sergt.	S.I.Y.
Peach, H. E.	Private	K.S.L.I.
Peach, J.	L/Cpl.	K.S.L.I.
Peake, J.	L/Cpl.	K.S.L.I.
Plant, J. T.	Private	N. Staffs.
Poole, C. C.	Corpl.	S.I.Y.
Poole, T.	Private	27th Canadian Regt.
Poole, W. E.	Private	K.S.L.I.
Poole, H. W.	Corpl.	Herefords
Poulter, G. H.	Private	K.S.L.I.
Poulter, C.	Private	K.S.L.I.
Powis, T. A.	Sergt.	K.S.L.I.
Price, R. H.	L/Cpl.	K.S.L.I.
Price, W. W.	Private	K.S.L.I.
Price, C. H.	Private	West Yorks.
Pritchard, A. W.	Corpl.	R. Fus.
Pritchard, J.	Private	K.S.L.I.
Pye, T. H.	Private	K.S.L.I.
Ramsell, H. C.	L/Cpl.	R.W.F.
Roberts, A. J.	Driver	R.H.A.
Robertson, W. W.	Gunner	R.G.A.
Rogers, G. W.	Private	Lancs. Fus.
Roberts, C. S.	Private	R.A.M.C.
Rowson, G. E.	Private	K.S.L.I.
Russell, J. R.	Private	Cambridge Regt.

Shenton, E. N.	Private	N. Staffs.
Skidmore, R. C.	Rifleman	Rifle Bde.
Sankey, D. E.	Private	K.S.L.I.
Scarratt, G. W.	Private	K.S.L.I.
Shuker, D. E.	Private	S.I.Y.
Slaney, J. C.	Lieut.	R.F.A.
Smith, R. H. B.	L/Cpl.	K.S.L.I.
Smith, P.	L/Cpl.	R. Berks.
Snape, S. G.	Private	Lancs. Fus.
Spicer, T.	Rifleman	R. Irish R.
Spencer, T.	Private	Labour Corps
Stokes, W.	Private	K.S.L.I.
Swift, H. H.	Private	K.S.L.I.
Swift, T. W.	Private	Herefords
Taylor, C. A.	C.P.O.	R. Navy
Thomas, W.	Private	K.S.L.I
Thomas, E.	Private	R.W.F.
Thomas, A.	Private	M.G.C.
Thomas, A.	Private	M.G.C.
Thomas, B. I.	Private	K.S.L.I.
Tipton, B.	Private	K.S.L.I.
Tomlinson, W.	Private	Worcesters
Vaughan, W. E. H.	1st A.B.	H.M.S. Vanguard
Waltho, H. R.	Private	Middlesex Regt.
Weaver, A. E.	Private	K.S.L.I.
Welsby, R.	Private	K.S.L.I.
Weston, J.	Private	R.W.F.
Wicks, F. W.	Drum-Major	R. Warwicks
Wicks, J. H.	Pioneer	R.E.
Wilkinson, P.	Corpl.	K.S.L.I.
Williams, J.	Private	K.S.L.I.
Woodfine, C. S.	Gunner	R H.A.
Wood, W. G.	L/Cpl.	K.S.L.I.
Wood, T.	2nd Lieut.	West Yorks.

" As dying and behold we live."

II Cor., VI Ch., IX v.

Lych Gate Memorial plaques

served as the Independent Conservative MP for the Wrekin and unveiled the plaques in this capacity. The scandal overshadowing the the Lych Gate Memorial was brought to light after the dedication ceremony in 1922. Unfortunately Townshend's war record, although appearing to be exemplary was somewhat less than honourable.

Major General Townshend was famous, or perhaps infamous, for commanding the 6th Army Division of the Indian Expeditionary Force (IEF).

The discovery of massive oil deposits in Mesopotamia (now Iraq) and neighbouring Persia (now Iran) was timely for the Royal Navy as they were busy converting their massive naval fleet from coal to oil power, thereby giving the area vital strategic

Major General Townshend

importance. In November 1914, Allied troops began landing in Mesopotamia with the intention of securing the oilfields and refineries from Ottoman Turkey who had joined the Central Powers led by Germany on 28 October. When the IEF arrived in May 1915 and moved towards Basra, it was split into two divisions at the Tigris and Euphrates rivers.

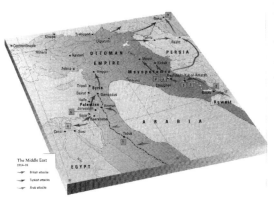

Mesopotamia - scale map - 1915

General Sir John Nixon tasked Townshend and his column with fighting their way up the Tigris and capturing Baghdad. This was not only the Ottoman headquarters but also the terminus of the Berlin-Baghdad railway. Capturing this Mesopotamian capital was therefore seen as a way of hitting back at the Germans by defeating an ally and undermining the stalemate on the Western Front. This battle strategy was masterminded originally by Winston Churchill. It was designed to defeat the Ottoman Empire, which was controlling Turkey and most of the middle eastern region.

Initially Townshend's campaign met with modest success, achieving some objectives on the road to Baghdad. His supply lines grew longer as the Turks' became shorter but without reinforcements his men grew

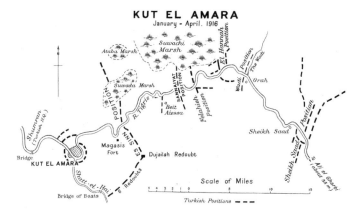

Scale map of Kut-al-Amara and Baghdad - 1915

weary and succombed to the climate and disease. By September 1915 they had captured Kut-al-Amara and by November, they were only 24 miles from Baghdad when they met strong resistance.

The Turks had been able to reinforce their troops from the failed Gallipoli campaign and were now superior in numbers. The expedition lost momentum and failed spectacularly in a welter of indecision on Townshend's part whether to consolidate his victories or capitulate. His army numbering 8,000 men fell back to Kut where in April 1916, they were surrounded and captured. He had faced the might of a vast Turkish army led by a wily old German, Field Marshal Baron von der Goltz, who was in the service of the sultan of the Ottoman Empire.

Townsend and his army were interned by the Turks. Apparently he spent the rest of the war comfortably housed in Sultan Mehmed V's villa located on an island near Istanbul. There, he threw lavish dinner parties and indulged his passion for conducting elaborate yacht races. Townshend's men however, were not so lucky. They suffered great hardships under their Turkish jailers and less than half of them made it home at war's end. It was reported that their Turkish captors had systematically tortured and executed them. Although it was every serviceman's duty to attempt escape and repatriation back to the war to resume the fight, Townshend's behaviour was overlooked. There were no attempts to court-martial him on charges of treason and neglect of duty and it was speculated that this was due to his rank and well-to-do background. The aristocracy and powers that be closed ranks when one of their own erred. This was a time when rank and privilege were the dominating factors in English society. In 1920 he resigned from the Army and had the gall to write a war memoir called *My Campaign in Mesopotamia*, presumably to vindicate his dubious war record. When news of this scandal finally broke it spelled ruin for Townshend, who died in penury and disgrace in 1924. When probate of his will was published that year it listed his total assets at just £119.

Wellington's Other Monuments to Victory

After the war it was decided Wellington should form an ex-servicemen's association called Comrades of the Great War. It was conceived as a club for the benefit and welfare of local veterans, dedicated to their interests and well being. To this end, a clubhouse and

Sir John Bayley Club today

recreational facilities were built on Haygate Road.

Eric Evans (father of George Evans - who earlier described Eric's involvement in the war) was a founding committee member. It was established with support from the government to counteract the influence of two other ex-servicemen's groups with more radical political agendas, that had sprung up in the wake of post-war discontent at the treatment of veterans.

Nevertheless, they all aspired to the same basic goals: better pensions and recognition of the needs of former soldiers. All these splinter organisations would merge in 1921 to form the British Legion.

Wellington College founder Sir John Bayley became involved and as a local benefactor and philanthropist he purchased the Comrades of the Great War club. In recognition of his benevolence, it was renamed the Sir John Bayley club, a name it bears to this day. It was also opened to all men, irrespective of war service.

One of the more curious monuments to the Great War was the First

First World War tank in Bowring Park

World War tank that was erected in Bowring Park and became a tourist attraction.

This was not a mock up but an actual tank (complete with serial number) left on display for park visitors to ponder over. It was left in situ right up to the 1930s when it was removed to make way for new flower beds and then mysteriously disappeared. It was possibly sent for scrap as times were austere then due to the Depression. Today, it would be in questionable taste to put such a war trophy in a public park for children to play on. Although historically significant, relics such as these are now consigned respectfully to museums for the benefit of people to learn about the past. In those times it was viewed as a public reminder of conquest and valour in battles against great odds and of a world war which the UK and her colonial Allies had helped win. This tidal shift in attitude illustrates how differently Britain regards war today and the change in public perception of what statehood and civic pride means.

The Mayor of Wellington's Response to the War

In 2014, a century after the start of the Great War, Wellington commemorated the local people who had sacrificed lives and livelihoods. Councillor Karen Tomlinson, Mayor of Wellington made the following comments:

On 4 August 2014, important events were held in Wellington to commemorate the outbreak of the First World War which started exactly a century ago. The re-dedicated remembrance plaques on Wellington's Lych Gate War Memorial still bear witness to the significant number of local people who made heroic and personal sacrifices. In doing so, they changed the face of the town forever. Small, developing businesses were destroyed, land use was changed, families were irretrievably broken and often, their property was lost forever. The lives of almost 200 townsfolk were taken. From this terrible suffering and tragic loss, the town began to witness a gradual shift in social thinking. The aftermath of this terrible war gave rise to changes in views and attitudes in the minds of those left behind.

Among these were changes to thinking about democratic rights and responsibilities and these helped to lay the foundations for the democracy we all enjoy today. However, these were only foundations. Many challenges, which had been temporarily sidelined during the war, quickly reappeared. The suffragettes were given a partial victory but their voting rights were restricted to women over thirty years old. It was not until 1929 that all women over 21-years-old were enfranchised.

'Many men who fought in the trenches had also been denied a vote because the franchise had been restricted to male householders only. The subsequent legislation which gave to all men over 21-years-old a vote was a great victory.

So at the time of the Great War, many had no right either to vote or to participate in local democracy by holding public or civic office. I'm sure you will agree the subsequent granting of this freedom was long overdue. Undoubtedly, it has created enormous and incalculable modern benefits. The office of Town Mayor I enjoy today has developed from this refreshing, democratic thinking. In a modern world, opportunities are now available to all who wish to pursue political careers at local and national level and of course, I applaud this.

However, after the war and following all the new thinking, a number of perpetual questions still remain. Was the utmost price for victory paid by so many still worth the paying?

Such sentiments reflect the enormous strides in forward thinking made by the citizens of Wellington and indeed the UK as a whole. We must keep in mind that at the time of the Great War, Britain was perceived to be an unstoppable and mighty imperial force empowered by God to give the Germans 'the thrashing they deserved'. In this post-colonial era of the Commonwealth, Britain is now regarded as the voice of mediation and well-intentioned civility. The days of 'gunboat diplomacy', once perceived by Great Britain and most other European countries to be the only solution to international disputes, are long gone. Fortunately, the political circumstances that gave rise to the outbreak of the First World War are thankfully consigned to the wastebasket of history.

Yet a sobering thought lingers. No future global conflict will be fought in long lines of trenches laid across vast battlefields populated by huge armies. It will, however, be decided simply by push-button remote control deployment of the latest technologically-advanced weaponry.

The 2014 Centenary Commemorations in Wellington

On 4 August, 2014, the author was invited by George Evans to attend a special commemoration service that he was hosting. It was conducted outside the smart new civic and leisure centre complex off Victoria Road, the refurbishment of which is testament to the thriving nature of the town in the new millennium. The ceremony was well attended by townsfolk and civic dignitaries including Mayor Karen Tomlinson and Town Clerk Howard Perkins.

The proceedings commenced at 10.00 am and were designed to reflect the enormous diversity in population and religious creeds that make up not only this Wrekin Town but the whole of multicultural UK.

George Evans read some poems about war, recalling its brutality and ultimate futility.

He then introduced Mia Cunningham, holder of the title Young Shropshire Poet Laureate. She gave her own poetic rendition of her generation's attitude to all wars. This was followed by peace songs

First World War commemoration ceremony at Wellington Civic and Leisure Centre, 4 August 2014

from local talent David Rolfe and peace poems read by local poet Jeff Phelps.

George concluded the ceremony by reading prayers for peace for the Sikh, Buddhist and Muslim communities who also sacrificed their own precious blood when the call came for volunteers from across all the British colonies. Each country answered in their thousands, resulting in 2.4 million men dead, wounded or missing.

Wellington's civic forefathers would have approved heartily as would their fallen.

Their dreams of freedom from tyranny are now realized and evident in Britain's democratic laws.

The commemorations moved on to take in the main First World War memorial sites across the town, commencing with the Lych Gate Memorial at All Saints Church on Church Green,.

It is appropriate to begin with this monument as the full tally of war dead are inscribed on its brass plates and the original main service of commemoration was held there in 1922.

Lych Gate rededication ceremony, 4 August 2014

British Legion - Lych Gate Great War commemoration ceremony 2014

Representatives from the local branch of the British Legion invited visitors to plant a commemorative marker (comprising wooden cross shape and poppy) to the fallen in a special configuration, marking out the letters and numeral of 'WW1' on the adjacent lawn.

Each contributor wrote on the marker the name of a relative who fought in the war and planted it into the display, which ultimately comprised dozens of poppy tributes.

The poppy as a symbol of commemoration was first introduced by American Moina Michael in the 1920s. She was inspired to wear a poppy after reading John McCrae's classic war poem, which reads as follows:-

In Flanders' Fields [1915]
In Flanders' fields the poppies blow
Between the crosses, row on row,
That mark our place, and in the sky,
The larks, still bravely singing, fly,
Scarce heard amid the guns below.

The Haig Fund was set up in 1920 by the eponymous C-in-C of the BEF who never forgot his men and was deeply concerned for their welfare post war.

Lych Gate - British Legion commemorative wooden poppy markers - 2014

It was designed to care for ex-servicemen and when the British Legion was founded in 1921 the fund was absorbed into the charity and retains its name today.

The Legion launched the annual poppy appeal to raise funds around the time of Remembrance Sunday and Armistice Day. Although initially settling on the colour red (after the Flanders Poppy) white poppies were sold during the 1930s in a bid to represent conciliation. The popular red colour was restored after the Second World War.

Other monuments visited on the commemoration tour of 4 August 2014 included St. Patrick's Catholic Church which boasts a memorial crucifix statue and plinth with plaque. This church was the first to raise a First World War memorial and was dedicated in 1920. The 23ft high crucifix and plinth was erected following the fundraising efforts of its own congregation. The inaugural service on 14 August was widely attended and officiated by local aristocrat Lord Stafford. It was dedicated to the nine Catholic servicemen (including brothers George

St Patrick's Church, Wellington, First World War memorials

and Joseph Healey) and all the men of Wellington who perished in the war.

Dedicated by Sir John Bayley in memory of his wife who died in 1928, the chapel at Wrekin College (formerly Wellington College) contains the memorial plaques to all the old boys fallen in the war. There is also a central display table of Stuart Hodgson's effects including the bible donated by his mother.

(See plate in Chapter 5) - Stuart Hodgson and bible at Wrekin College Chapel. The Old Hall School Chapel was dedicated as a war memorial to all the old boys killed in the war and was consecrated by the Bishop of Lichfield on 21 October 1922. This chapel is now a private house off Holyhead Road. Brass plaques recording the names of the fallen were relocated to Wrekin College Chapel. The First World War memorial plaques are now located in the entrance lobby of the school's new site. (As mentioned in Chapter 5: see relevant plates)

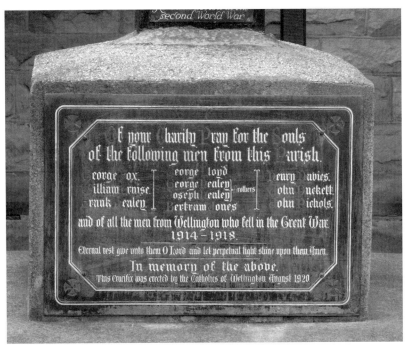

St Patrick's Church - First World War Commemoration Plaque

The Memorial gates at Wrekin College on Constitution Hill were a gift from Sir John Bayley in 1927.

Located on Chapel Walk off High Street, Wellington Christ Church

WWI Dedication Wall Plaque contained within Wrekin College Memorial Chapel

WWI Memorial Plaque shown on Wrekin College Gates that were commissioned by founder Sir John Bayley

(Church of England) contains a screen with associated plaques. Forming part of the rood screen it is an extensive structure, stretching back into the nave.

Wellington's Annual Armistice Day Commemorations

In Wellington, the town's fallen are commemorated every Remembrance Sunday and on Armistice Day on November 11. George Evans officiates the ceremony with the current dignitaries from church and civic authority, supported by members and flag bearers of the Wellington branch of the British Legion. Even though he is increasingly frail, George, who is in his nineties, attends every year. His contribution is central to the proceedings as he recites the Ode of Remembrance from Laurence Binyon's poem *For The Fallen [1914]*

They shall grow not old, as we that are left grow old: Age shall

Wellington Christ Church WWI interior memorial side-screen plaques

not weary them, nor the years condemn. At the going down of the
sun and in the morning, we will remember them.

The Peace Garden - a Wellington Man's Quest

It is surprising to discover that no country or official organisation has
established a simple commemorative place dedicated to the concept of
universal peace. It is all the more remarkable that it should fall to a
citizen of Wellington, George Evans, to create a Peace Garden to
celebrate the fact that for the past seventy years, we have not seen
conflict on a such a global scale. George takes up the story:

'It occurred to me that we have any number of gardens and parks

dedicated to the commemoration of war up and down the UK and also across the world. Yet the simple idea of celebrating peace in this way seems to have passed us all by, explains George. *'So, I decided to campaign for some suitable public land locally.*

I was eventually granted permission by Wellington Town Council to utilise an area of the civic garden space outside the newly refurbished council administration and leisure complex off Victoria Road, near the town centre, for this purpose. Besides the beautiful flowers and plants on public view, we also display inspirational poems by local and national writers that will hopefully plant other kinds of seeds in people's hearts and minds for generations to come.'

A Final Afterthought

The most commendable gesture towards world peace and reconciliation comes from one of the town's oldest denizens; the nonagenarian George Evans. A teacher, writer, journalist, historian and chief recorder of the social history of his beloved Wrekin Town, he is not just a truly magnificent example of what makes a great Wellingtonian but a great Englishman as well. He is also the closest

George Evans at work in his Peace Garden

surviving link that we have to that lost generation so tragically affected by the Great War. A man whose own father fought in that war and who is himself a veteran of the Second World War.

It is therefore fitting that we should let him have the final word on the subject of warfare. Perhaps George is echoing the sentiments of his own father Eric and those of that sage-like Great War veteran, the late lamented Harry Patch, when he utters the following short but cryptically apposite epithet:

War is stupid.

Index